CELLULAR TRIANGLE

By

PAUL SWIST

∞ INFINITY
PUBLISHING

All rights reserved. No part of this book shall be reproduced or transmitted in any form or by any means, electronic, mechanical, magnetic, photographic including photocopying, recording or by any information storage and retrieval system, without prior written permission of the publisher. No patent liability is assumed with respect to the use of the information contained herein. Although every precaution has been taken in the preparation of this book, the publisher and author assume no responsibility for errors or omissions. Neither is any liability assumed for damages resulting from the use of the information contained herein.

Copyright © 2012 by Paul Swist

ISBN 978-0-7414-7478-0 Paperback
ISBN 978-0-7414-7479-7 eBook

Printed in the United States of America

Published October 2012

INFINITY PUBLISHING

Toll-free (877) BUY BOOK
Local Phone (610) 941-9999
Fax (610) 941-9959
Info@buybooksontheweb.com
www.buybooksontheweb.com

This book is dedicated to my mother.

In memory of "Zorro"
June 16, 2002 to July 9, 2009
Rest well my son.

PROLOGUE

Time passed, and it was no secret about this so-called "investigation" of me. In the beginning of 2008, I've let it be known to different officers of the courts for reasons of my past history. Do I have any regrets? By no means. My past is just stories. But, sometimes in life, an individual will use one's past to his own advantage... to justify his so-called "investigation."

No man who reads this story can say they lived the way I did. It's unheard of. I truly believe I was chosen by the man upstairs to bring this to light.

Over time, you have seen bad coaches, priests, teachers, and law enforcement officials cross that line. The dirt always comes out. Maybe not right away, but at some point down that dirty road, the dust just lingers, and a world of awakening comes about.

April 8, 2008
To: Joyce Oliver, Esq.
From: Paul Swist

Dear Ms. Oliver:

This correspondence includes a variety of items -- my comments, phone records, and an audiocassette tape -- regarding a serious matter that I would like you to review. To this day, I have an identity theft/fraud issue with my Sprint wireless account. It came to my attention in December 2007. I was not receiving my bill from Sprint and, upon my looking into the matter, I was told that it was being sent electronically to an e-mail account with the address ---@yahoo.com. Needless to say, that is not my address, as I do not have an e-mail account. I brought this information to the Lower Origin Township Police Department, Sherman County, PA, in December 2007, and spoke to Detective Leons. I explained to him that I believe I knew who had committed the fraud and stole my account information. When I explained to him how I had figured it out, he was impressed by my reasoning. Since I had already contacted Sprint, I passed on the phone number and any pertinent information that I had already discussed with the Sprint representative. I was upfront with Det. Leons, as I had been in the past, and as you will read in the following paragraphs.

I went to the police station in the third week of February 2008. I spoke to a Detective Mitch and asked him to have Det. Leons touch base with me and let me know what, if any, progress was being made with my case. His reply was that Det. Leons was on a wiretapping case and unavailable. Again I touched base with Det. Leons on March 10, 2008. I went to the Lower Origin Police Station again and asked to see him. He was able to speak with me; we went into his office and he told me he was unsure as to what kind of crime had been committed. I told him I believed that someone was using my identity to set up an e-mail account and have my personal phone information sent to their own account, and that it had to be some sort of identity theft. After I persisted with this point, he said he had sent a subpoena to Sprint for the records, but that he had never received a reply. I then told him I believed it was a federal crime to use someone's identity fraudulently. Det. Leons told me to call him on Wednesday, March 12, 2008, and, with hope, he would have some information for me. I called on the 12th and left a message for Det. Leons, to which I received no reply. For your information, when I was with Det. Leons last, he walked me out of his office and said "Oh, by the way, I ran into your probation officer." I just shook his hand and left. I am not sure as to the intent of Det. Leons's comment but I am concerned that my fraud case is not being taken seriously and that the person or persons who set up the fraudulent account could be doing it to others. Perhaps they could be involved with worse things, like child pornography. Moreover, I believe that this is a personal vendetta against me by the person who set up the ---@yahoo.com account; what if a child were to be abducted? What if I was right and these people are doing this to more people than just me? Is Det. Leons willing to accept responsibility for that? I am not sure why the police were not interested in tracking the IP address of this account; this would have eliminated any uncertainty.

I assume, Ms. Oliver, that Det. Leons isn't being upfront with me. You see, I met an escort girl this past summer; her name is Betty Rico. Her call name is Lavender. I did not fully realize what I was getting myself into. Things got pretty heated over the course of our first episode. She wanted me to "whack" her boyfriend. She told me his routine and how the job could be done. She said he was a drug dealer, selling weed and ecstasy. She wanted him dead because he was hitting her at the time. I told her not to tell me any more. On July 1, 2007, I got a text message from her stating "I am going to do something crazy and I need help." Another text came through that said "I need to talk to you." I tried to reply to her but received no answer. I tried her home phone number and got no answer there, either. I did not know where she lived. I went to the gym and ran into one of my friends (who is a Lower Flanagan Police Officer), Pat Marm. I outlined my worries to him. He explained to me that it would be nearly impossible to track down a judge on a Sunday to get a court order for a trace of Lavender's cell phone-- she would probably be dead by the time it could be accomplished if she was in the level of danger I feared. He said he was sorry. I tried calling again-- this time, she picked up. I told her she scared me because I thought she would slash her wrists or kill her boyfriend.

The second episode occurred when she claimed she was pregnant and that I was the father. I thought about the situation and made the decision that I would take responsibility for the child even though I was not sure whether I was its father. I made a preemptive move by telling her that she had to change her lifestyle and I extended her the offer of moving in with me. I had found her a job making $40,000 a year with full benefits. This is when our relationship got bitter. I decided to contact her mother. We text messaged each other and spoke on the phone. Her mother appeared to like me. She said Betty had told her about me. After a few more days of text messaging, I found out her mother did, in fact, know about her daughter's "other side." I believe she was profiting from it. My concern, though, was for the unborn child's safety and well-being. I received about five more text messages from her mother. I told her that her daughter was immoral and a wackjob and that she should go to the Sitwell Police Department and describe to them how she had wanted me to "whack" her boyfriend. Because the episode took place at my house, I also felt

I had to go to my Township Police Department and report it. That is when I met Det. Leons. I told him the whole story. I reemphasize that my primary concern was for the child Lavender said she was carrying. Det. Leons asked if I would wear a wire. I said I would, but the problem was that I no longer saw the woman. Later, I came to find out she was not really pregnant.

I have another friend at the gym, Ms. Oliver; his name is Francis Yannucci. He is second-in-command of the Sherman County Narcotics unit. I have known Mr. Yannucci and his wife for 20 years. Francis and I work out. Around mid-July 2007, I brought to Francis Yannucci's attention the situation about Ms. Rico. I told him what I explained earlier in this letter: that I had told Det. Leons about the drug dealing boyfriend, how he could be reached, and so forth. I even went as far as to tell him the best and safest way to find Betty's boyfriend, as he is her driver. In the meantime, I gave Francis information about her; he got back to me and told me that he ran a check to find that she has never been arrested. He told me he has her picture on his desk. A couple of weeks after that conversation, she froze her cell. Francis and I discussed the situation and tried to figure out what was going on. We communicated at the gym and by cell phone. (Francis's cell phone, apparently, only accepts text messages and cannot send them.) I suggested to Francis that he check their Myspace accounts. He said he could not do that without permission to access their sites. I called again and suggested that he simply go to the Lower Origin library and check it out. He never returned my call regarding that issue.

On September 5, 2007, at 8:25, I sent Francis the following text message: "Francis I believe I pegged the cell # damn I am good." Three weeks went by and I heard nothing. On September 30, I ran into Detective Ben Wister. He is in charge of the Sherman County Narcotics Division. He asked me how I was doing and I told him I was well. I invited him to sit down and eat, but he had his kids with him. I did mention the situation with Francis Yannucci and asked him if he knew whether Francis was on top of it. His reply was that Francis is on it; Ben appeared to be in a hurry.

On October 2, 2007, at 12:07 PM, Francis called me and left a message. I called him back at 12:08 and we spoke. He said the cell number I gave him was a bad number. I asked him what he meant by "bad number," and he said that he passed the number on to his people who investigate such matters and, when they called the number, an unknown black girl answered the phone. He mentioned to me that it was the number of a law firm. I told him "no way" and asked if he was sure he passed the number on correctly. He replied that he did so. I repeated the number to him again and he said he would have his investigators recheck it.

On October 3, 2007, at 9:30 AM, I called Francis and left a message. Since I did not hear from him that day, I called again at 8:23 PM and got no answer. I wanted to speak with him, to tell him I double-checked the number, and it is, in fact, the number Lavender was using... but he never called me back to discuss it.

On October 5, 2007, I called Jake Slayback; he is an Upper Flanagan Township Police Officer. I talked to Jake a couple of times on the phone and once in person. I have known Jake for probably 17 years and have always felt that I could talk to him about personal matters. I also always felt he could tell whether someone was BSing him. I explained my situation to him and emphasized that I was not accusing Francis of fooling around; I just wanted his opinion, based on what I had told him. I asked him if he could call Ben Wister. He said he would and told me to call him back, so I left. A few days later, I ran into Pat Marm, the Lower Flanagan Police Officer, and I asked him if Francis had it in him to step over the line. He responded to me, saying, "Back in the day." We both went our separate ways and did our workouts. A couple of days later, Pat called me and said "he took it upon himself" to ask Francis Yannucci about my "stepping over the line" comment. Francis told Pat to stay out of the matter, that it was not his investigation and that he would file a grievance against him if he persisted.

Around the end of February 2008, I called Jake Slayback one more time, but he never returned my call, so I did not pursue the matter with him. I sent a text message to Francis Yannucci one more time on March 2 to apologize and I left a similar voice message with him. The following morning, I saw him in the gym and I apologized, for a third time, in person. I told him I thought he might have crossed the line because I could not understand why no one was following up on the apparent illegal activity. I again mentioned to him that Lavender was still using the same cell phone; I could tell by the music it played when it rang. He said to me "there are better things to cross over for." We started to go our separate ways when he made a final comment to me. He said "I have 450 guys under me. Who are they going to believe?" I said to him "You're right." A few days later, I checked Betty's cell number and it played a different song. I saved about six text messages from Francis Yannucci. I also saved text messages from Betty's mom, both incoming and outgoing.

Ms. Oliver, I never intended to get to this point. I have no cause for vengeance against Francis. I wanted to explain to you in some detail my relationship with him. I always gave him respect, as I continue to do to any law enforcement officer. I may be wrong in wanting to help a lady who got caught up in the fast lane. Back in the day, I would have handled the matter myself if a guy was slapping a girl around. People change and I realize it is the police department's responsibility to address these issues. Folks stereotype someone like Betty. I have learned from my past and I don't dwell on it; you always find out who your friends are. As you know, Ms. Oliver, we choose our own destiny, and no one takes our hand. I often wonder: In a courtroom, at the final sentencing stage, when the defendant stands, does he or she really feel sorry for the crime they committed-- or are they just sorry they got caught? I guess I have a soft spot in my heart for this girl. Eve tempted Adam in the garden. I guess, in this case, I am Adam.

The issue I have just outlined troubles me even more, Ms. Oliver, because of the involvement of Chris Marcus, a United States Probation Officer from the Wigfield office. You will recall that, earlier, I told you that his name was brought into my fraud case. I should explain what I believe is going on. P.J. Curtis and I were in a 15-year relationship that came into some serious problems a few years ago. For one reason or another, Officer Marcus felt that he had to intervene. Mr. Marcus made a number of comments and took what I consider to be "out of the ordinary" steps. For example:

1. Mr. Marcus came to the home P.J. and I shared in Mont Clare, PA. We sat down and he brought up the suggestion that, with the experience I had gone through, P.J. and I should not have sex anymore.

2. Mr. Marcus, in 2005 and 2006, informed me he was doing a six-month review and that he needed to speak to my doctor. I gave him my consent. For some reason, it has not happened again.

3. On July 29, 2005, P.J.'s birthday, Mr. Marcus called her at 9 AM, at her job, and then again at 9:05 AM, on her cell phone.

Officer Marcus was aware of P.J.'s health issues; she was seeing a psychiatrist and taking two kinds of medicine. I fail to see why he needed to have contact with her. I did not know Mr. Marcus had a degree in counseling. Let's just say that he was gathering information about me. If P.J. was pressured into lying and then felt guilty about making up a story, and were to commit suicide, is Mr. Marcus or his office going to take responsibility, or was he just trying to take advantage of her when she was not in a rational state of mind? What woman would want a probation officer calling her first thing in the morning on her birthday?

You see, Ms. Oliver: I went to Wigfield on July 28, 2005 to give a sample of my DNA. In the short conversation I had with Mr. Marcus, I mentioned I was taking P.J. out for her birthday (the following day). Again, Ms. Oliver, P.J. and I were having ups and downs like any other couple. P.J. is not a leader, but a follower. She is not a good liar but is an excellent manipulator. In the 15 years we were together, there was not one hospitalization report, not one police report, not one complaint from a neighbor. I have no recorded history of abuse until, at the end of our relationship, she went to the Upper Origin Police Station and claimed that I was beating her. I weigh 230 pounds and I said to the officer that she doesn't have a bruise or a mark on her body. His response was that he had to record the complaint anyway. P.J. would always say to me that I was good for only one thing. Ms. Oliver, you can use your imagination. I had to "perform" for her to get the tape that I am enclosing.

I realize I have included a lot of thoughts in this letter, Ms. Oliver, but I feel I need to protect myself and look out for my well being. Thank you and I hope to hear from you. You can call me day or night.

Sincerely,
Paul Swist

2

June 30, 2008
To: The Honorable Steven Marshall
From: Paul Swist

Dear Judge Marshall:

I bring this matter to your attention with reservation; I have been hesitant to contact you, but these issues go above and beyond "fairness" and for what our justice system is supposed to stand. The last time I stood in front of you, at my sentencing, you gave me a high commendation on the downward departure motions I had submitted to you. Your words struck me and have stayed with me. After my sentencing, I experienced a special moment and I told my mother that I would never let her down again. I have lived up to that promise to this very day.

When I sent the attached letter to Ms. Oliver, this information was not included. She may not have understood the full picture. If she did speak with anyone, she may have been told there was an investigation of me going on. If so, she only got a quarter of the whole truth. Your Honor (and Mr. Macnee): This is what actually happened. Someone substituted another female (who has been a friend of mine for four years) for Betty Rico in an attempt to entrap me. This individual's name and number were obtained through my cell phone records. She proceeded to engage in some sort of illegal activity that went on for a couple of months. If there was a legitimate investigation of me, should I not have been informed in writing that my phone was being monitored? Sherman County officials have again violated my rights. If you would like additional information on the details of this issue with the other female and any of the other tactics used against me, please feel free to call me.

As you know, Your Honor, sometimes there are people that hold positions of authority by virtue of their occupation or job title. We as citizens look up to them, respect and admire their positions, and grow to trust them over time. When we see these individuals cross the line for one reason or another it is, to say the least, disturbing. As I look back on the unethical behavior, violations of constitutional rights, and broken oaths of people sworn to protect all citizens, I am asking: Why?

The bottom line, Your Honor, is that there is probable cause for an investigation into what has happened to me recently. In 1999, I was being investigated by the Sherman County Narcotics division. I was served a document with the signature of Lance Pollack, saying I was under investigation for cloning cell phones. If I recall correctly, the document was also signed by a County Judge. I tried telling everyone involved I did not even own a cell phone at that time. What really happened was that the County Narcotics squad actually tapped my pager. The cloning issue was just a cover-up. In 2007, my cell phone usage and billing information was fraudulently obtained by someone. I never authorized the sending of my information to any e-mail account. I believe it is a crime to steal someone's personal information, is it not? There seems to me to be another cover-up. Has my past voided my constitutional rights? Are people, even those in law enforcement, allowed to use technology for their own personal gain?

Judge Marshall, I am requesting you not just to pick up the phone and ask questions of the people involved; I am asking that you look into the matter independently and fairly. As an example, you could just call Mr. Pollack (a former Sherman County DA) and ask him about me, but that would be wrong. Mr. Pollack does not know me; he has never met me, but he may say that I am an arrogant person because of what he has been told about me. To illustrate my point, I could say I know Mr. Pollack and that he has a stuttering problem. I say that based on watching a news conference one morning during which he was bombarded with questions that had caught him off guard. It was early in the morning and he probably had not had his second cup of coffee. My point is, Your Honor, I can't judge Mr. Pollack by that one interview; I am sure he is one of the sharpest tools in the shed, but he was not coming across that way that morning. I am asking that I not be judged by hearsay. Thank you for your time.

Sincerely,
Paul Swist

Enclosure
c: United States Attorney Michael Macnee

3

March 11, 2009
To: The Honorable Steven Marshall
From: Paul Swist

Dear Judge Marshall:

I address this letter of complaint to you for a number of reasons. My complaint is this, Your Honor: My probation officer, Chris Marcus of the Wigfield office, has been abused his authority in the past and continues to do so at the present time. Your Honor, I submitted this to you previously-- documents to show how Officer Marcus has been abusing his authority. The latest example occurred on the 19th of February, 2009. Mr. Marcus stopped by my residence and asked me to call him on February 23rd. I did this from a local pay phone. Mr. Marcus questioned me about one of my prescribed medications. He has been aware for the past seven years of the medications I take under doctor supervision. He asked me to give him a written explanation from my doctor stating the need for me to take this medication. I agreed and I met him at the Charlesville probation office, where I provided it to him, along with a urine sample. Mr. Marcus then proceeded to ask me about my other prescribed medications and why I did not have a letter from my doctor for those, also. I responded that he had only asked me for a single, specific medication. I also reminded him that he likely had my case file right in front of him when he and I spoke on the phone. His response was that he has 60 people to supervise and he can't remember what medications I am on. Your Honor, Mr. Marcus is aware of both of these medications; one I take for fatigue, and the other for joint pain. He went so far as to direct me to provide him with more documentation and stated to me that "we can do this the easy way or the hard way."

Your Honor, I hope you can see why I am bothered by the unprofessional behavior on the part of Mr. Marcus. As you know, the system is like a revolving door. Obviously I am doing well for myself but Mr. Marcus knows that my probation is almost up. We all see on the news about convicted felons with violent pasts inflicting harm or killing innocent civilians and police officers... and the judges get the blame. Maybe if probation officers weren't so worried about the personal lives of people not doing any wrong and staying out of trouble, nor continually ask for the same information about doctor-prescribed medications for documented health issues, and focus more energy on watching violent offenders, the region would be a safer place for all of us. If you would like more details on Mr. Marcus's blatant invasions into my personal life and that of my former girlfriend's, please refer to the letter I wrote in April of 2008 to Ms. Oliver that I subsequently sent to you. Mr. Marcus also affected my credit, Your Honor; attached is a copy of my credit report that shows the civil judgment on my record.

Finally, Your Honor, I want to reiterate the reason I don't have a phone. I had my cell phone bill pirated and no one from law enforcement would nor has ever addressed the issue.

Thank you for your time and I hope you can help with this issue.

Sincerely,
Paul Swist

POLICE DEPARTMENT
ORI: 0461700

Incident Investigation Report
09-1025 (01)

Incident Data

```
Class (UCR) Code: 7090 PUBLIC SERVICES - REPORTS          Complete
Crimes Code: Title:   C
Date/Time Reported:    05/30/2009 Saturday 10:31
Discovered Date/Time:  05/01/2009 Friday 08:00
Last Known Secure :
TIME - Received: 10:31 / Dispatched: 10:31 / Arrived: 10:34 / Cleared: 11:22
Badge:
Address:
   Landmark:
   Patrol Zone:
   Premise Type: HOME OF VICTIM - OTHER DWELLING
BIAS: 88 NONE (NO BIAS)
```

MO:
Weapon/Tools: NONE   Additional weapon:

Persons Involved

Number of Victims: 0   Number of Offenders: 0   Persons Involved: 1

```
COMPLAINANT          SWIST, PAUL A. (NP041846)
Incident Classif.: 7090 PUBLIC SERVICES - REPORTS
Type: INDIVIDUAL/PERSON (NOT L.E.OFFICER)        Injury:
Age/DOB: 46 03/07/1963  Race: W  Sex: M  Ethnic: N  Marital: S  Resdnc: R
SS#:
Height:   0 Weight:   0 Eye:      Hair:    Build:    Compl.:
GBM ID number:              Date Entered: / /    Date Released: / /
Comment:
OLN/STATE:                         /PA

Home:                          Home Phone:
Work Phone:            EXT:  Cell Phone:            Pager:
Employer:

DOCUMENTS ON FILE:
```

Summary

```
05/30/2009 12:05 Page 1 Ofc. 28
    ON THIS DATE, PAUL SWIST APPEARRED AT     P.D. AND REPORTED THAT HIS
911 PHONE SERVICE HAS BEEN BLOCKED BY AN UNKNOWN GOV'T AGENCY. HE BELIEVES
THIS SAME AGENCY IS MONITORING EVERY PHONE CALL TO AND FROM HIS CELL PHONE.
PAUL SWIST SAID HE BELIEVES THIS GOV'T AGENCY IS VIOLATING HIS
CONSTITUTIONAL RIGHTS.
    R/O ADVISED PAUL SWIST TO CONTACT HIS PHONE CARRIER FOR ASSISTANCE.
FURTHERMORE, R/O TOLD HIM TO CONTACT AN ATTORNEY REGARDING ANY
CONSTITUTIONAL RIGHTS VIOLATIONS.
```

Officer: Badge: Page: 1
Case Status: FURTHER INVESTIGATION   Case Disposition:
Approved: 06/04/2009 by:

United States District Court

for the

Eastern District of Pennsylvania

REC'D-PROB
2010 MAR 4 PM 3 33
USDC-PHILA

FILED
MAR 5 2010

U.S.A. vs. Paul Andrew Swist   Case No. 2:01CR00011-001

Petition on Supervised Release

COMES NOW ▮▮▮▮▮▮ U. S. PROBATION OFFICER OF THE COURT presenting an official report upon the conduct and attitude of Paul Andrew Swist who was placed on Supervised Release by The Honorable ▮▮▮▮▮▮ sitting in the Court at Philadelphia, PA, on the 19th day of April 2001, who fixed the period of supervision at eight years, and imposed the general terms and conditions theretofore adopted by the Court and also imposed special conditions and terms as follows:

ORIGINAL OFFENSE: Attempt to possess more than 500 grams of cocaine with intent to distribute (Count One).

ORIGINAL SENTENCE: The defendant was sentenced to 48 months custody of the United States Bureau of Prisons with a 8 year term of supervised release to follow.

SPECIAL CONDITIONS: 1) The defendant shall participate in a drug treatment program which may include urine testing at the direction and discretion of the probation officer; 2) The defendant was ordered to pay a fine in the amount of $2,500.00 at the rate of $100.00 per month; 3) The defendant shall pay any financial penalty that is imposed by this judgment and that remains unpaid at the commencement of the term of supervised release; and 4) The defendant was ordered to pay a special assessment of $100.00 due immediately.

RESPECTFULLY PRESENTING PETITION FOR ACTION OF COURT FOR CAUSE AS FOLLOWS:

Mr. Swist has had numerous contacts with the ▮▮▮▮▮▮ Township Police Department. The contact has raised concerns regarding the subject having mental health issues based upon the following:

On July 27, 2007, Mr. Swist reported to the above police department. He informed the police he

RE: Swist, Paul Andrew
Case No. 2:01CR00011-001

was involved with an escort service. The relationship involved the escort trying to have him involved in a murder for hire plan.

On December 16, 2007, Mr. Swist again returned to the above police station to report suspicious activity regarding his sprint cell phone account. He stated the phone bills for his account were being sent via e-mail to an unknown source. The incident resulted in him not receiving any statements since August 2007. The subject informed the police someone; possibly a prior female acquaintance, was keeping track of his calls in an attempt to disrupt his personal life.

On May 30, 2009, Mr. Swist again appeared at the ███████ Township Police Department. He reported that his 911 phone service was being blocked by an unknown government agency. He believed this same agency was monitoring every phone call to and from his cell phone. Mr. Swist informed the police that the government agency was violating his constitutional rights. The police advised the offender to contact his phone carrier for assistance. He was further advised to phone an attorney regarding any constitutional rights violations.

On August 1, 2009, Mr. Swist again reported to the above police station in reference to listening devices in his home. He informed the police that listening devices were illegally installed in his apartment. Mr. Swist claimed the devices were triangulated from satellites that orbit above his home. He stated the devices were monitoring every sound he makes and controlling his cellular phone. Mr. Swist informed the police that he discovered the devices using equipment that he built. According to the subject, his equipment is able to pick up the high and low frequency signals. Mr. Swist indicated that "someone from the county," he refused to say who, is responsible for the installation. Mr. Swist was very vague in describing why someone would want to install such equipment and refused to give any names of the parties involved. During the conversation with the police, the subject advised there is a strong magnetic field coming from his ceiling. The interviewing officer noted, in his opinion, the subject might be experiencing some mental health issues.

It is recommended that the special conditions of supervision be modified to include that the defendant shall participate in a mental health program for evaluation and/or treatment as approved by the Court after receiving a recommendation by the U.S. Probation Office. The defendant shall remain in treatment until satisfactorily discharged with the approval of the Court.

RE: Swist, Paul Andrew
Case No. 2:01CR00011-001

Mr. Swist declined to sign the modification and informed this officer he has no need for mental health treatment. He has requested to have a hearing before the Court, but refused to sign his name on the forms.

PRAYING THAT THE COURT WILL ORDER... **THE ISSUANCE OF A SUMMONS DIRECTING THE NAMED SUPERVISED RELEASEE TO APPEAR AT A MODIFICATION OF CONDITIONS HEARING.**

I declare under penalty of perjury that the foregoing is true and correct.

Respectfully,

████████████████

Supervising U.S. Probation Officer

Place Reading, PA
Date February 22, 2010

AW/am

ORDER OF THE COURT

Considered and ordered this 25 day of Feb, 2010 and ordered filed and made part of the records in the above case.

████████████████

ICC: Detention

4

It's Sunday morning. Mother's Day. I check my cell phone booster as usual. I am still in the triangle, just as I have been for the last 10 months or longer. I know Francis can't throw in the towel yet. Why? Too much manpower has been invested. A whole lot of money and ego.

It's me against technology and Francis and his stooges. As the months go by, I keep my character and composure intact, because that's all I have.

At one time, my cell phone used to be close to me. Then, things became unusual and out of the ordinary, especially because I am a very routine person; an individual who pretty much keeps to himself. It's when I started to connect the dots, when people would make different gestures toward me to get information of some nature, when I told myself, "It's Francis!"

I'm sure Francis told them not to overkill the subject. Francis knew from the past and present that I am very alert, but I played along to a certain extent. I would use old-school techniques and be patient. My mom used to say "the more bees you have, the more honey." I had to see who was on the up-and-up. So I did the "whisper thing." That's when you tell one person one thing and wait to see who repeats it. It's got to be sweet, so you can see the bees buzzing. I knew this wasn't going to end anytime soon. Not by me, not by Francis. This was personal.

I mentioned all of this to my older brother. He's a family man. Also, I showed him all the documents. We ended up in a heated conversation. He also asked me how much medication I was taking.

"I believe in 'respect!'" I replied back.

I am a person who lives by that. It costs no money. Some of his words still linger in my mind. A priest once said to me that he'd rather get smacked with a brick to the face than with harsh comments.

I also mentioned this to my workout partner. He was more aware of the situation. He is a highly-educated person who graduated from Cornell University. He started to see the dots connect, but he said, "Paulie, think about it. They have to be spending a lot of money."

It didn't take much time for it to sink in with me. I noticed for a few days in a row that he didn't bring his cell phone to the gym. I didn't say anything to him at first. All I know is that I've known him for 17 years, and he always brought his cell to the gym. I just laughed.

I'm only one guy, and I am ready to outwit them.

At one point, I couldn't understand how they were getting the jump on me. Was it when I was purchasing my new cell phone? Was there a GPS unit in my car? Was I followed, or was I too routine?

The stores from which I purchased phones were K-Mart and Wal-Mart. The difference between the two was their return policy. Wal-Mart had a 15-day return, while K-Mart had a 90-day one. I was at the K-Mart more often. TracPhone was my choice at that point. I would use all of the prepaid minutes and then return it. Upon my doing so, the cashier would ask me if there was anything wrong with it. I would say I wasn't satisfied. It was then that I said to myself that this was getting old. Then, I came across Net 10 service. Upon activation, it would provide 300 minutes. I was in Heaven.

But not so fast, I thought. I still had to figure out how they were getting my cell number so efficiently.

My memory is sharp. I would see individuals around me when I was in the stores. I noticed what they were doing when I purchased the cell-- they were observing precisely which carrier I'd chosen.

When I would activate the phone, I would always use a pay phone. I'm not saying that's bad; it's just that I had no other phone to use. After I gave the information required, which only took about eight minutes, the new phone was good to go. At that time, I realized a free text message comes to your cell phone with your number.

I understand the cell phone towers somewhat. I was using common sense, for by no means am I an Einstein. I knew they were pinging my cells every time I purchased one. A day or two later, a number would indicate an incoming call. Well, I caught on to that. Also, Francis's nest wasn't too far from my residence. I had my boy check for me the location of the closest tower. It was nine-tenths of a mile away. The tower was owned by the county.

I said to myself, "That's just fuckin' great!"

So as the weeks and months went by and the letters to different officers of the courts received no response, I thought they could have sent me a letter and lied to me, at the very least. Again, I said to myself, "It is what it is!" I went about my daily routine, which is mainly working out, eating six to seven times a day, and being a father to my Rottweiler, Zorro.

Everyone who knew me knew I was a true dog person. Some people I knew would say, "You wanna talk to Paulie? Don't talk about working out-- talk about his dog. He'll talk all day about Zorro!" I can honestly say that he kept me focused throughout this bullshit.

I had to keep my sense of humor. No way would I show weakness. Yes, things do happen in life. Some are natural and some are horrific, but you have to move on toward what may be a new challenge.

And so, with Francis still making my life as miserable in every way they can, I am locked on it like a cruise missile.

CELL PHONE BOOSTER

5

  The house in which I live was probably built in the 1940s. It's been converted into three apartments. I reside in the finished basement. I call it my "hut." It is small, but it serves its purpose. I moved there for the yard. Zorro weighed 179 pounds. He needed his space, if you know what I mean.
  There was a young couple in their 30s with a child living directly above me. I chit-chatted with them every once in a while. They know a little about my past life in the fast lane. There are two driveways shaped like a horseshoe. The couple always parked their vehicles on one of the driveways for a couple of years, and that's how it always was until this one evening. I noticed they switched driveways but didn't think much of it. Then, on a second evening, their car was again in a different spot, close to my apartment. I didn't say anything, but I did see his demeanor change when I said, "I read people pretty good." Afterwards, he started to press me for my cell number. At that time, I was flipping my cells. It struck me just like sciatic nerve pain shooting down my right leg. I got it! What he was actually doing was

maneuvering his van closer to my cellular antenna. In my hut, if you don't have a cellular signal booster, you won't have service.

Let me take the time to educate you on this device. It works off of two different networks: CDMA and GSM. The frequency range is 1,850 to 1,990 MHz (PCS only). My unit has an antenna and a 120-volt AC power outlet along with an R-6 cable in the back. This leads to an outdoor antenna.

So Francis persuaded another person, my neighbor, to go against me, and I understood now. It was a "high tech" government issue. Millions of dollars in equipment involved.

As I'm writing this down, I think to myself, *This all stems from a piece of ass!* I should have listened to my mother years ago when she said "Paulie, you should date an Amish girl." I thought that notion only jocular-- oh well!

A few weeks later, my neighbor informed me that they were moving. I played along with it, saying, "Yeah, you probably need more room, anyway, for your child." They packed up their stuff and jetted off to their new residence. Before that, he stopped by a couple of times and asked me for my cell number, but I just gave him some BS story. I was cool about it. I went about my routines.

Then, one day, I took some of my crazy-wear sweatpants to outfit them with new elastic. I've been to this dry cleaning place four or five times in the past. I dropped the pants off and asked the woman behind the counter how much it would cost. Eleven dollars per pair.

"Fine. When can I pick them up?"

As she handed me the receipt, she said, "In a week."

I then asked if I could use her phone. It was a landline. I dialed one of my cells. I hit *67 to hide the number. I knew that Francis was watching that cell, so I had to make it look good. I had to put some of that honey out there. Well, it worked! They took the whole jar.

Anytime a lady or someone got in touch with me, Francis would follow up and tell them some BS. A regular citizen will get tunnel vision when approached by law enforcement. Everybody knows I am a convicted felon. So, who are you going to believe? Two and a half months go by and my sweatpants were not done. Every time I stopped in, she would say, "I didn't get to them yet, Paulie." I would just laugh to myself. Finally, I told her to let me have them back, and I walked out the door.

As the game continues, I feel like I'm playing a combination of Clue and chess with "Mr. Francis, with the laptop, in the office." On the other hand, I have to be careful not to be checked or checkmated. As I observe my cell phone booster, I got a couple of ideas.

I took a drive over to Lowe's to purchase 50 feet of R-6 cable. Later that evening, when it was dark, I said to Zorro, "Daddy gotta work!" He would be sitting, always on the lookout, or sprawled out like a big bear rug with his eyes shifting in every direction. If he heard something, he would let out a heavy bark, his nose wet, catching any pheromones in the air.

As I was attaching the R-6 cable to my booster, I decided to pick a spot in front of the house where there was a small tree. It branched into a Y-shape about waist-high.

"Perfect!" I said to myself. I placed the cell booster in the tree, then plugged in the extension cord needed to "turn on the juice." Luckily, there was an outlet out front, so I didn't have to purchase a longer, 100-foot cord. I checked everything: The booster was in place and I left the antenna in the original spot, where Francis was locked onto it.

"It's time, Francis. You and your stooges."

I turned the booster on and saw it flicker with green lights every time a car went by with a driver using a cell phone.

Now, Francis thinks those cell numbers are mine. About 15 minutes went by. I started to see different cars acting out of the ordinary, especially this one car with tinted windows. It stopped for about 10 seconds, then took off at a rapid speed.

"Francis's goal," I say, "is to get my cell number." And when that occurs, they'll find a way to intervene in my life and that of my females.

The next morning, as I was pulling out of my driveway, I saw a custom van parked across the street. I didn't think much of it because the house right next to mine was for sale. Its landscape has basically the same layout as my house. I continued down the road, then turned around and drove back. I saw the guy on his cell phone. It just seemed odd. Something wasn't registering in my mind.

That evening, I decided to elevate Francis's blood pressure again. After I hooked everything up, the booster wasn't flickering. I checked and rechecked. Then, I flashed my shit-eating smirk, the one I used to give my ex-girlfriend. I had figured it out. The dude from that morning was giving different coordinates to his stooge brothers. So, once more, I drove over to Lowe's to purchase a 25-foot R-6 cable and a 25-foot extension cord.

Later that evening, I repeated myself to Zorro, "Daddy gotta work."

I ran the extension cord and the R-6 cable all the way down to the mailbox. I said to myself, "I can't stand here with this object flickering." I put the trash can right next to the mailbox and set the booster on top. I turned it on. The smirk returned to my face. I saw the cars flying up and down the street again.

As I put more thought into this bullshit, I said to myself, "Motherfucker! The landlord! That scumbag!" It was then that I understood. If people were to move into the other apartments upstairs, that would mean they'd have more friends and family over, and more cell phones. Francis couldn't monitor around all that.

A month passed and the landlord stopped by. He was taking care of some odds and ends. He's a BSer and believes he's a good one.

So I played him. I said to him, "You don't have anyone looking at the apartments?"

"Just low-lifes," he replied.

My landlord lives about a half an hour away. As I was small-talking with him, he asked me for my cell number. I didn't give it to him at that point. I wanted to toy with him just a bit. I suggested to him that, instead of him driving here, I could show the apartments to anyone that would be interested. He responded by saying "I don't want to inconvenience you."

"No biggie," I told him.

"Okay."

He was still piddle-paddling around and exhorting me to give him my cell number. As I turned and walked away, I got that smirk on my face. I gave him a number, all right. I gave him one I knew Francis already had. I was watching him, and I saw his expression. It was like he knew he had pulled something over on me. I got into my car and left, saying to myself, "Now, how am I going to show apartments without any keys?"

A few days went by. I called him and told him I knew this lady who was interested in moving in, but that she'd like to see inside. He responded by telling me to have her call him. I agreed.

I didn't hear from or see him again.

6

    I wanted to be extra sure. Seeing is believing. If I was ever going to be able to bring this to a courtroom, I would have to be able to justify my issues. So I focused on this lady at the gym. It was wrong, and it bothers me to this very day. You may say to yourself that I had a choice, but at that time, I was simply on a mission. For what it's worth, I apologize to the father and his daughter.
    Every day I saw this guy (whom I'll call Bill) at the gym. Before I know his name, 10 months went by. I used to talk to him about football, weight training, guy stuff, and his daughter. I could tell he was a good man-- very humble and respectful. I could also tell that that's the way he raised his family. So, every time I saw him at the gym, I would call him "boss," "chief," or something like that.
    Let me tell you, I am a person who is very bad with names, be they male or female. There were times when I would walk into the gym, see a girl, and she would look back at me, waiting for whatever name I would call her. As I looked at her, I would think

to myself, *No, it begins with* this *letter.* I'd blurt a name out when I crossed her path. She'd just shake her head, probably saying to herself, "Decent looking guy, but none too bright." From then on out, I just called her "Hon."

Finally, one day, I asked the gentleman for his name. He said it was Bill. And I replied, "That's easy." After that, every time we met, I would say, "Hi, Bill!" He would just give me a polite smile and we would go about our workout.

Now, my mom usually sends me a gift card for Christmas. Fifty dollars or so. I'm not much of a shopper, so I had this card sitting around. I said to myself that I'd put it to good use by giving it to Bill's daughter. I knew she was a respectful person, just like her father. So, when I passed the card to her, I gave her my cell phone number with it. I also told her the story about my mother giving me the card. I mentioned there were no strings attached. I smiled and walked away. Later that evening, at around 10 PM, I got a text message saying, "Hey, it's ---. I wanted to say thank you again. That was very sweet. You didn't have to. I think I will go do some shopping tomorrow night."

As Francis was monitoring my cell, he thought this was an escort girl, since it read like I gave her extra money to go shopping. I could tell that, afterward, Francis got to her and then to Bill. Some more messages came after that. I texted back, but had to press the issue a little harder to get what I set out for. So, when I saw Bill at the gym, I would press his buttons. He just wouldn't give in. I guess Francis told him they would handle it. I'm sure Francis put in a good word for me.

One day, at the gym, I guess I struck a nerve, and it was eating at Bill. He got off his machine and asked me if I had a problem.

"Come on," I replied. "Be serious."

"You know!" he said. "You know!"

I got what I wanted, but there was no smirk on my face. I just walked away with my head down. I knew I was in the wrong, but if I ever had my day in court, they would both have to be subpoenaed.

7

Sometimes I feel like I am in Oz. I've got courage and at least three-quarters of a brain. Maybe that little wizard dude behind the curtain could provide me with a fourth character who has a set of balls. By that, I mean a lawyer who won't be intimidated by Francis and his stooges.

One of the many times my probation officer stops by, he acts like he doesn't keep in touch with Francis. He's predictable. It's like reading a Dr. Seuss book, he's so easy to read. He would ask me, "Do you think I lose sleep over you!?" I'd just give him that look of mine and say "Whatever." He would respond by telling me he'd be in touch. Then he'd slowly go down the driveway, shaking his head, just like all the rest.

So, as Francis was still up my ass, and I couldn't figure out how they were following me, I came to understand about command post from my past. What is it, actually? It's when the team is at different locations in your area or your residence and they are just hovering to blend in. There have been occasions when I've been somewhere and spotted one or two. I'd think to myself, *No way!*

So I started to check my car. I've never seen a GPS unit before, so I really didn't know what I was looking for. I merely understood how they worked. Each day I would check a spot on the car and say to Zorro, "Daddy gotta work." I didn't realize how many spots could be on a car.

"This is fucked up!" I said. "I gotta get more input! Education!"

When I used to go to Target once in a while to get a cell phone, I noticed they had GPS units. I bought one, knowing I was going to return it. But before returning it I decided to methodically tinker with it. I charged it up and read the directions. That's something I never do because I am too impatient. This, I had to do.

So I got my tape recorder. It's one of those types into which you stick a little tape. I was a bit familiar with magnetic fields. If you turn on the recorder near different components, with or without a tape in it you will get a transmitting frequency. Each signal is different. I did a couple of my own tests with a microwave oven. It made one noise. My cell phones had a unique sound to them. Net 10 and TracPhone had a good, loud sound. My Motorola phone, from the very beginning, had a distinctive sound to it.

The GPS was charged up. I turned it on and, at the same time, I activated my recorder. The recorder picked up the three short beeps and then I noticed my cell phone booster flickering. I thought to myself, *I thought GPS worked off of a satellite. Maybe this worked off of cell towers.* I was more interested in the beeps it put out.

I returned the unit and got more input on GPS devices. I looked in the Yellow Pages and found a guy in New Jersey who dealt in counter-surveillance. Each of the three times I spoke with him was from a different pay phone. Eventually, he informed me that it would cost $400 to do a five-procedure sweep of my vehicle, consisting of TSCM services, a physical check, RF-detector sweep, magnetic leakage sweep, and a motion RF sweep. We agreed on an early Sunday morning appointment, and I gave him my address.

On that Sunday morning, I got up early, around 4:30. My adrenaline was kicking in. He arrived around 8:00. We met on my driveway. I rushed to him and quickly gave him his $400.

"Come on!" I said, hurried. "Come on!" I didn't want Francis to shut down if he was spotted. I didn't want to take any chances.

I let him do his thing. He walked around the car. I said, "I got you, motherfuckers!"

He took off his headphones. "Nothing, Paulie."

"Are you sure?"

"Yes," he replied. Then I asked the dude about the flashes on the cell phone booster, and he couldn't give me an answer. I went numb. Something wasn't adding up. My mind started to backtrack, and I said, "That's it." He gave me one of his business cards and said to call him if I had any questions. I went back in the house to take a leak. I was looking out the window, trying to put it all together. Then, it dawned on me.

Francis somehow manufactured a situation. They took it to a judge to get a subpoena for the pay phones I was using. They were monitoring them. So I shake my johnson and flush the toilet.

"$400 down the drain." I thought Francis got me good on that one, but I vowed never to express or show it.

8

People and animals share the same instincts. They prey on the weak. You may think that, when a pride of lionesses are out hunting, they're using Nextels to communicate.
"Hey, Cat One, this is Cat Two. Cat Three informs me of wildebeest 50 yards ahead. That's our target." The lioness just knows the wildebeest can't disguise his character, but I can.

As events went along, I learned that the main detective contracted a tumor behind his eye, and he was claiming to have lost his sight. I let it be known that this was due to karma. Well, that didn't go over too well. I heard he was pissed. One day, I was at the gym, and he happened to be there, too. I was talking to some chick with blond hair. In order to see in the direction where I was standing, as he was walking, Francis was forced to turn his head and look over. That let me know he could see me. So, as the bee hive got larger and dripped with honey, I needed a little more information. I needed to understand their signal to my antenna.

One night, I ran the R-6 cable to the third floor window on the side of the house. I went back into my hut to dial a number. I could see my cell phone booster flickering. That told me they were trying to pinpoint my antenna. Early the next morning, as I was taking a shower, I heard this guy say, "There it is!"

The next night, I buried the cable. It was cold that night. The cable wasn't flexible, but it served its purpose. I got the same reaction as I did with my booster. The next morning, I went to the gym. When I arrived home, I took Zorro out and noticed that the cable had been dug up.

"Predictable," I said.

As long as I am in the triangle, Francis can pinpoint my antenna. One day, I wanted to get a number that had been on my old cell phone since the very beginning. I turned it on and placed it on the wet bar. I was cleaning and heard the voicemail chime. I did a double-take. I disconnected that cell many months ago. I was puzzled. I didn't know what to think.

A couple of days went by. I stopped over at my boy's pizza place. I've known him for at least 20 years. I grabbed a couple of slices and he sat with me. While we were shooting the breeze, he mentioned to me that I called him the other day. It had been a missed call.

"Dude," I said, "I didn't call you." The last time I could remember calling his cell was when we went to a Flyers game a few years prior. He looked at me. I said, "See?" He knew bits and pieces of what had been going on. At that point, he covered up his cell phone with a newspaper. I just gave him a polite smile and nodded my head.

Later that evening, I decided to do a little homework. I called Sprint using my old cell. I couldn't dial out on it but I could hit *2 and get customer service. I played it that I wanted to reactivate my old number, and I also wanted to know whether the same number was available. When all was said and done, I had been transferred to three different people. No one could give me an answer.

"What could Francis be up to now?" I asked myself. "I know!"

What Francis was actually doing was searching. That means they had to somehow go into the archives to see with whom I associated. For this reason, I believe Francis thought I may have had someone on the inside, feeding me information, because I was always one step ahead.

As time went by, I kept in touch with my older sister. She knows a very little bit. It was too deep to discuss with her. When I did call her, she had caller ID. A name would show up: Yardley Fletcher. He knew I would figure it out. That was his way of telling me. Of course, as my sister, she was concerned just like any good sis should be. I told her that it all stemmed back to that one escort girl.

"Don't they have anything better to do?" she asked.

"They have, easily, six figures invested in me."

Soon after, my cell read "call ended." They would always pull those tactics.

9

For the record, the first name of the second-in-command of the stooges starts with "F" and his last name starts with "Y."

Along comes Super Bowl Sunday, every guy's time out, including my own. As I get ready to watch the game with Zorro, my satellite dish flashes to my screen "Technical error. No need to call service."

I thought to myself, *This is fucked up!* and said to Zorro, "Daddy can't catch a break."

This went on for an hour. Finally, I walked down the street, looking for someone who has a dish mounted on his roof. The guy who answered the door looked like a loyal football follower, so I asked him whether his signal was coming in from his satellite.

"Clear as day."

I shook his hand and I apologized for bothering him.

"No problem," he said.

I turned and walked back to my hut. As I was walking, I spat on the ground, thinking, *That's okay... that's okay. I'll have my day.*

It was just like the past, with the same pattern, and the same bullshit. Francis's tactic was to get my new cell number, which would then renew the subpoena. During this process, Francis could intervene in my life or endeavor to set me up with an escort, then bust me for soliciting. That way, they would have the right to come into my hut, hoping they'd come across something illegal. I've seen that move from day one.

You should be careful what you wish for, Francis.

10

    I know this is all out of the ordinary, but I am a person who believes in standing up for himself. The following morning, when I woke up, I said to myself, "This is really fucked up." I made it a mission that morning to get a response-- little did I know! I got a shower, dressed, and ate my Cheerios as usual... but instead of going to the gym, I went to the township police station. It's only five minutes away. I've been there many times before. They all know me. The heavy-set dispatch guy behind the bulletproof glass was there. Before, when I used to go up there, he would say, "He's back." I could read his lips.
    When I walked in, I asked, "Is Chief in?" He asked me what this was about. I told him it was a personal matter. He rang the Chief.
    "What can I do for you?" asked the Chief. I wanted to tell him to get his boys off my back.
    The Chief asked me to have a seat. I asked him if we could have a little privacy. I knew the little fat guy would be zeroing in. So the Chief invited me into his office. At the same time he asked

me to have a seat, I was asking him whether he was aware of the complaint I filed against one of his detectives.

"No."

"Are you sure?"

He told me he wasn't aware of it. In the past, with previous issues, I've passed information on to the Chief about someone stealing my own info.

That day, I informed him that my residence was being triangulated. After I said that, I mentioned that maybe there was someone being investigated near my home, and the signal was bouncing off of their roof into my place. At that point, I couldn't keep a straight face.

"Look," I said, "I don't care about that system. I've got nothing to hide. I am here today because I basically was able to decipher how that system works." I told him my cell phone booster was one-way. I mentioned that I could jam it up. I knew that the only time it had shut down was because of a computer virus on the day before April Fool's. I also knew when it was on auto or manual, and also how many seconds it took to ping my cell.

He said that if anyone has the system on my house, they would have had to have gotten a subpoena. I told him I was there to help him with the system.

"I am inviting you or whomever to come to my residence, so I can explain it," I said. "I know this seems odd, but I have better things to do." I told him the system had been on my house for a while, and I learned about it by using various methods. As we wrapped up our conversation, he said there would be an internal investigation and that he'd call in two days. I shook his hand and thanked him.

"You boys are in trouble," I said as I walked to my car, "now that Chiefie is involved."

Two days went by and no Chief. So I headed back to the station. You would think I was a cop for as many times as I was there. I asked the little fat guy if the Chief was in. He rang the phone and told me the Chief would be right out.

"Look, Chief," I said, "I don't wish to bother you. I just want to resolve this." He asked who I thought was doing this. I named a couple of detectives, mentioning that they even text-messaged me.

"They do what?" the Chief asked.

"Text me!"

I told him about messages I sent. One was a text saying "Someone been upstairs." A message came back reading "Someone been downstairs." Another message sent to me read "identify yourself or i shoot you in the fuckin head." Still another said "Do you swallow?"

He asked me how I knew someone had been upstairs. I told him that there were certain marks I had put on the doors. He asked me if I still had the text messages, and I replied in the affirmative.

I said to myself, "Francis was used to me returning the cell phones, but this one cell, I never returned." I sent Francis many text messages, taunting him. He couldn't resist when I put a thorn in his side. I used it to my advantage, to show in court if I ever got my chance.

The Chief told me that he and another person were going to stop over.

"Okay," I said. "Just give me a little bit of time to get my dog set up." As I was sitting in my car, he came over to inform me that he'd have to get back to me. I had also wanted to inform him about my mail being tampered with on a couple of occasions.

That time, I got the runaround.

11

One time, I sent a high-profile lawyer in Philadelphia all of my documents. I waited to hear from him. A week or so went by, so I decided to call him. He basically told me he wasn't interested. I thanked him anyway. I let a few more days go by and then I checked my mail. I never received my documents, so I called him again.

"Sir, you told me you were not interested in my case, but on the other hand, I've not received my paperwork back."

He said he would put it in the mail that day. Again I thanked him. Three days later, I got my paperwork back. Usually, a lawyer will attach a front page to it. I thought that maybe he does things differently, but what caught my attention was the documentation of the original response I received from the state police. I could see that what the lawyer had sent me was a photocopy. It was sloppy. I also saw stapler marks made from a copier machine. Again I called him.

"Sir, I know you told me you weren't interested in the case, but what I received back from you was a photocopy."

"I sent you what you mailed me," he replied.

"Okay." And I left it at that.

Another time, when I sent documents to a firm, I talked to my boy at the gym about how many stamps it would take. We figured it would take at least three or four. I had already sent it out with six stamps. About a week later, I checked my mail. I saw in the mailbox the same envelope with "return to sender" stamped on it. I noticed there were two stamps missing.

Fuckin' assholes! I thought to myself. I could see on the envelope where someone had peeled off the stamps. My boy and I always thought there was some kind of listening devices at the gym. Francis would pull any kind of tactic against me, and this was their way of letting me know.

So another day arrived: More attitude from me, and persistence followed. On this day, I decided to call the FBI. Maybe a little fat guy would answer the phone. I was getting pissed, but the honey was dripping and the bees were buzzing.

The morning didn't side with me. So, I figured I'd try mid-afternoon, after I was done working out. The only thing that bothered me was that I didn't have a clean cell. Francis could intervene as they had in the past. It's like they say: If you don't try, you'll never know.

Maybe Francis and his stooges are at the Dunkin' Donuts and they can't monitor my cell phone.

So I got the number for the FBI from the phone book and gave them a call. An agent picked up. I asked with whom I was speaking, but the person said he couldn't give out that information. I said "Okay." No sooner did I start to explain my situation than he put me on hold. About 45 seconds passed by, and I knew what was up. Net had broken into my phone conversation, as they had done so many times in the past.

When the FBI agent returned to our phone conversation, I explained to him briefly that someone from Sherman County was abusing their technology by tapping into my prepaid cell phones. I also informed him that I figured out their system. I knew when it was on auto or manual. I knew that the only time it had been shut down was due to a computer virus.

As I was talking, he cut in and said, "Look. If I bought a prepaid cell, it would take at least two weeks before we could get the ENC number."

"Yeah," I said, "but I am followed, for when I purchase a cell it is immediately followed up on."

"You would have to be an Einstein to figure out cellular technology."

Well, I thought, *I must be Einstein reincarnated.*

So much for calling the FBI.

LEGAL AID OF ▮▮▮

ADMINISTRATIVE OFFICES,

PLEASE REPLY TO:

October 6, 2009

Mr. Paul Swist

Dear Mr. Swist:

I am the attorney assigned to review your case. Please call me at ▮▮▮ extension ▮ to schedule an appointment.

Very truly yours,

SLS/af

Friday, October 16 @ 10am

LEGAL AID OF ███

ADMINISTRATIVE OFFICES

PLEASE REPLY TO:

April 15, 2010

To Whom It May Concern:

Please be advised that Paul Swist was seen in our office on April 12, 2010 for a landlord/tenant issue. Unfortunately, we cannot provide any assistance to Ms. Swist at this time.

Please feel free to contact me if you have any questions.

Very truly yours,

AMF/s

12

One time I pulled a slick one on Francis-- a real curve. It was one of my test methods. I looked in the Yellow Pages, under "Escorts." It was 5:34 AM. I knew Francis would be in a deep sleep. But I wouldn't put it past him; when he goes to bed, he isn't counting sheep. I dialed the number. It rang about four times.

"Good morning," a voice answered. I chuckled, then hung up. I knew whose voice that was.

Not that it really mattered, but as a few more days went by, one evening, I checked the cell phone booster. Sometimes I would just use the recorder and listen for the signal to go out. It was good if I heard the noise within 10 to 15 seconds, but, in another way, it was bad. I would usually punch in 2s, 3s, 4s, etc., and press "send" to see how the booster reacted. That particular evening, anything I punched into my cell read "No Service." I tried repeatedly.

What Francis was wishing for again was for me to use one of my good cell phones. Francis set the system up to block this particular cell phone. So I said, "Okay. Playtime! It's like Romper Room." I got my old Motorola and reset my Net 10 cell by simply removing the SIM card and replacing it. Simultaneously did I turn them both on. The signal went back to their system and showed that there was a cell phone in the triangle. This reset their System. (Let's say there is a home invasion. I couldn't call 911. I would have to go through that whole process just to place an emergency call.)

The next day was a Saturday morning. I went up to the police station. The little fat guy was behind the window, as usual. I thought, *Everything is routine; why not this?* I asked whether the Chief was in.

"Nope."

"Is there a sergeant?"

"Nope."

"Is there a corporal?"

"Yes," he responded, "but he's out on the road. I can radio for him to come in and he can make out your complaint."

"Thank you," I said.

As I was waiting, I felt like I was playing a game of Wheel of Fortune. The little fat guy was Pat Sajak and I was just a contestant. "What's next?" I ask.

The officer arrived. I shook his hand.

"What can I do for you?" he asked.

I told him my complaint was that I couldn't dial 911 because I was triangulated in. I told him how my living quarters were set up. I tried to explain to him a little bit, but I have learned from the past that, if you give bits and pieces, people will look at you kind of funny, like you're a wackjob.

The officer knew me from my past, and we had also gone to school together. He was concerned, but there wasn't much he could do apart from writing out my complaint. I thanked him and told him that I understood. We shook hands again.

I went out that revolving door one more time, thinking to myself, *Well, it's better to go out with your hands at your sides than behind your back.*

13

As weeks turned into months, I heard through the grapevine that Fay was doing "deep cover" work. You may ask yourself why I call him Fay. During this escapade, I used to get a massage at least three times a week, sometimes more. My back used to bother me a lot. There's this advertising circular that used to be delivered to my house every Wednesday. I used to read the massage advertisements like the stock quotes... until I got wind of Fay's plotting. When I started to see things out of the ordinary, my back started to feel a lot better. Then I had this gut feeling. I knew it. There was one ad for a massage therapist and her alleged name was Fay. Let me remind you that these initials are those of the guy in charge of the stooges.

About a month went by and I still read the massage advertisements, but I did not call. Then, one Wednesday, I just happened to be outside when the circular was delivered. The dude didn't chuck a paper at my driveway, but I could see the circular flying through the window to the other driveways.

For the 20th time, I said to myself, "You assholes!"

Fay was second-in-command of the Narcotics Squad in Sherman County. He was highly respected among his peers, with well over 1,000 drug convictions. When I would see Fay at the gym, he would only be there until 11 AM. He went and did what he did best. On Sundays, he would teach other law enforcement officers tactics working with state-of-the-art technology. He was elite at his job. If Fay was locked on you, there was no passing Go. You would be locked up and there was no Get out of Jail Free card. When Fay contracted a tumor that impaired his vision slightly, that forced him to be immobile.

He still held his rank, but then he started the Deep Cover project. I guess that, due to the economy, the County wanted to prepare for increased crime. So Fay put his team together-- the stooges. His intentions weren't directed at helping the community. He had a plan, and his plan was me. He was going to make an example of me. Little did he know, Fay compared me to his other flunkies, who thought with their dicks.

Yes! Females will make males weak and vulnerable. So I kept my zipper shut and didn't cross that line. In the beginning, when Fay and I were friends, I brought a video of this girl and me to show him. She was a hottie. So, as Fay and I were fast-forwarding the video, Fay said, "Get to the coochie." She had a nice one. As time was getting short, we jetted out of the gym and went our own ways.

The only reason I ever bought a video camera was to film Zorro and my hut so that I could mail the discs to my mother. Well, here was another lesson learned. I made one too many different movies with one too many different females. All the discs looked alike. I would call my mother once a week after I mailed one to her. Each week, when I called, she would give me a different story -- like she's been busy or didn't get a chance to hook up the DVD player -- stuff like that. Finally I realized what I had sent her.

"You dumb fuck!" I said to myself.

Oh well-- it was what it was. We never discussed the disc situation again.

14

Now, you would think, since I have two drug convictions -- one state and one federal -- that I would have an attitude against law enforcement. My mind doesn't work that way. So let me elaborate for you and use this as an example: Let's say a few guys from the Narcotics squad are working out at the gym and some wackjob comes in with a gun, firing at them because of a past altercation. One of Fay's boys is hit with a piece of lead and he can't move. Now, I don't want to be a hero, but I am going to do what I believe in. From where I'm positioned, I'm thinking, *I can drag him to a spot where he'll be safe.* As I lunge to grab him and start pulling his body along the floor, I feel this burning sensation in my thigh. I hear Fay's voice yell "My back! Friendly fire!" as I am dragging the Narcotics dude to safety. I say, "Your old lady on her back, and it's just a friendly fuck."

As you watch the news, priests, teachers, and officers of the law can all cross over a line. Does that mean that none of them can be trusted? No. It's just that some of them think that they can abuse their authority. If Fay didn't wish to get involved when I brought the issue to his attention, then he should have told me instead of playing me. Then I wouldn't be writing this. As I said in the very beginning, I believe in respect. Now, if Fay wanted to get his wiener off, that's his business, but BS me and try to play me? Well, then I'm going to burn him.

Now that Fay was out to get me, I supposed he would approach my ex-girlfriend to get some information. I could only imagine what she would say: "Find Paulie's money and he'll bleed. That's how you hurt him." My ex and I were together for 15 years. Believe it or not, when I met her, she was also a highly-paid massage therapist, if you know what I mean. She also had a legitimate job. I got her out of that one predicament. It was like that movie *Pretty Woman*. She was an attractive female, very humble, but she was also a spitfire. Zorro was another reminder of her. We had purchased him together. She taught him some of the things that he had come to expect and enjoy, like tugging on a rope.

Every evening, we played "tug tug." It also cleaned his teeth. But, one evening, Zorro's demeanor changed. He was bleeding from his upper gum. I didn't think much of it because I just figured that the rope had scraped his gums. Another day went by and I came to see little pockets of blood. So, on the third day, I called the vet. The vet couldn't fit him in, so I called a specialist. They quoted me a price of $400 simply to look at him.

"For $400," I said, "you will *do* something for him." I called my original vet back and said "Look. I think Zorro has a cavity or something wrong with his upper tooth." The office told me to bring him in the following morning and not to feed him after 8 AM. I voiced my understanding and thanked them.

That morning, I dropped him off and headed back home to wait by the phone. I was anxious to pick him up. Around 11:30 AM, I got my call, but it wasn't to pick him up.

"Paul?" said the lady veterinarian.

"Yes?"

She stuttered at first, then: "It's bad. It's real bad." She went on to say that his teeth were fine, that she had even cleaned them, but what was occurring in Zorro's system was that his platelet levels were at zero. At that, I interrupted her to ask what would have caused that. "Rat poison," she responded. My mind went dead. Silence! She quickly entered back into conversation by saying "As we speak, we have Zorro on three different antibiotics, and Prednisone." She wanted to monitor him until the evening.

So, as I was driving at 6 PM to go and retrieve my son, my stomach was knotted up. I felt like I could take someone's life in the blink of an eye and not have any remorse over it.

But, ultimately, Zorro pulled through.

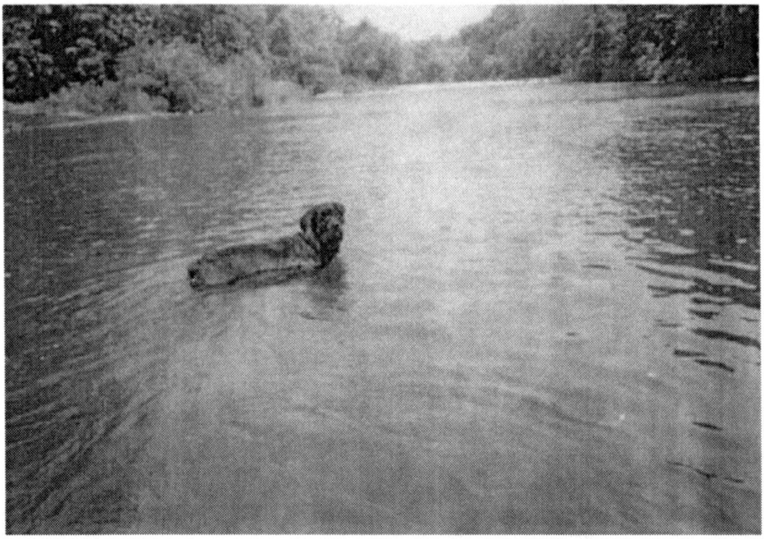

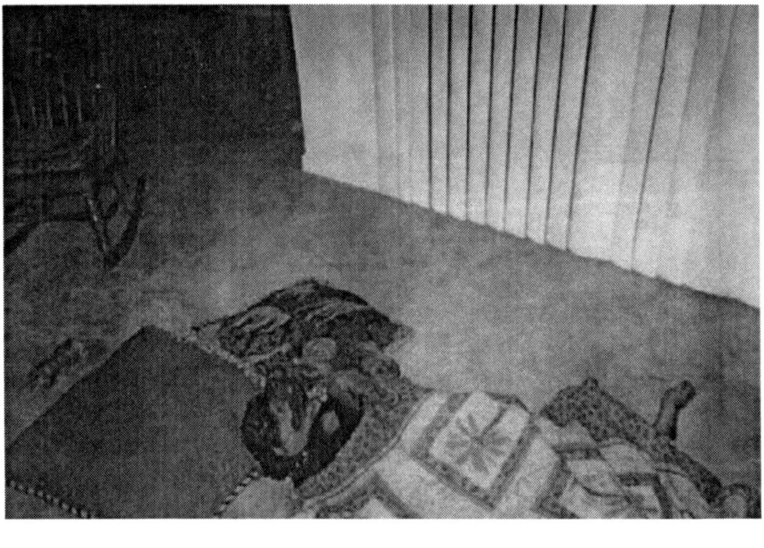

15

As Fay's mind was working and using his law enforcement abilities to its advantage, I played right along with it, employing head games. Anything I would text, he would read. I chose those past habits of his of which I was aware to toy with his mind. I also had to let him see me on his video. My body language couldn't show weakness. That was forbidden in my eyes, but, in reality, there were days during which I got really frustrated. But then I would snap out of it, usually by writing, working out, and keeping positive.

So another day went by and I had this notion that Fay knew I had tried to obtain different lawyers. He monitored my mail. He poisoned everybody around me and there wasn't a damn thing I could do about it.

"Okay," I said. "So I'll bring the people into the triangle... and their cell phones, too." I made up a sign that read "Antiques Yard Sale." To the sign, I added "Stuff from the 50s, 60s, and 70s." I posted it two weeks before the yard sale. I listed my cell phone number after a "for more information" notice. But I made the numbers small so that, when you drove by, you could see the sign but not make out the cell phone number. That meant you would have to drive into the triangle to write it down. Now, you know how people love antiques. At the very bottom, it read, "Ask for Fay."

About a month had gone by since the dude came up from Jersey to scan my vehicle and basically fuck me. I decided to call him. But, before I punched in his number, I bet myself that he would say "Hold on-- I've got another call." So I punched in his number and pressed "send." About 45 seconds into our conversation, it happened. Fay interrupted the call just like all the other times. About a minute later, the guy from Jersey switched back over to me and said "Paul, you're trying to play technician." I had put him on the spot, and he knew it.

Fay knew he had gone over the line in the beginning with the dude, but it was the same old song, repeating over and over. Now, I am an understanding person, and I can relate to why Fay was ticked off at me. He got caught messing around with a whore. Everything and everybody to whom he spoke said "I'll handle it. I'll make an example out of him." The list goes on. Fay invested well into six figures on me. To top it off, I figured out their multimillion-dollar triangulation system, he contracted a tumor, and I wrote a book.

After I hung up with the dude, those three-quarters of a brain I have were saying "They want me to think I'm being paranoid." *What?* I thought. *I guess they think I'm one of Jerry's or Oprah's kids.* (For the record, I respect what Jerry Lewis does for the handicapped and what Oprah represents to the children over in Africa.)

A few more nights go by. I heard Zorro growl twice, then bark deeply. He looked at me. I could see his ears tuning in like a shortwave radio. He slanted his eyes at me. There was somebody upstairs.

I turned down the television's volume and listened for someone to walk or come in unnoticed. You would have to weigh 50 pounds; the house is old, the floors are hardwood, Zorro doesn't miss a trick, and me? Well, I notice everything. After a little bit, I sent a text message: "Someone be upstairs." A message came back saying "Someone be downstairs."

"You assholes," I said to myself. "Sooner or later, something's gotta give. This is getting old."

I was so used to Fay's routine and his so-called "tactics;" I didn't even need the cell booster anymore. I would just turn the tape recorder on and I could tell what was going on by distinct sounds. I did know one thing: There would come a day when it would shut down. I always had this thought that if I could reverse it and send some sort of energy burst to burn their system, it would be better than any message. Oh yeah!

Father's Day was fast approaching and I guess I was a dad. I had a 160-pound, furry son. On that afternoon, my brother stopped by-- maybe to check up on me, maybe to shoot the breeze. What I did know was that our last conversation was pretty heated. One of the things he had mentioned was that, once I locked on to a situation, I don't stop. How right he was. So, as he hopped off his Harley, I greeted him, but I also said to myself, "Seeing is believing," meaning now I was able to demonstrate and ask him for his opinion. In my mind, I knew he was very hard to convince. As I had said to him in the very beginning, "Read the documents very thoroughly." The bottom line? He didn't. So, as we went into the hut, I asked him to remove the battery from his cell phone. He gave me that Swist look and I gave it right back. I was anxious to ask him what he made of a magnet stuck to the ceiling.

About a week before he stopped by, I was standing near the wet bar, holding up one of those earth magnets I use for the arthritis bracelets I make. I had it near my head to see whether I had removed all the Krazy Glue. At that split second, it shot out of my hand and stuck to the ceiling. I gave it a 10-second stare and that three-quarters of my brain started to gear up. I had a bunch of earth magnets. I started to put them all over my ceiling, but I couldn't understand from where the energy was coming.

What is doing this?

I was determined to find out. I got my Hitachi 18-volt drill and attached a 1 3/4" drill bit. I picked a spot on the ceiling to drill. The drywall was one inch thick. I thought that that was unusual, so I started to shine my Maglite through the ceiling. I couldn't see any metal-- just wooden rafters. Then I started to put a metal rod in and I probed around... still nothing.

The next day, I went to a sports store to purchase a compass. As I gave the cashier my money, I thought, *It is Friday, 5 PM. Most people are out with their loved ones, enjoying a nice evening out to dinner. And here I am buying a fucking compass.* I went home thanking my mom for sending me to Scouts, because now I know that, wherever I am, a compass is always going to point north... unless there is a magnetic source inches away.

Back in the hut, I stood perfectly straight and I held the compass waist-high and facing north. I lowered it to my knees and needle remained stationary. Then, I raised it over my head, next to the ceiling, and the needle began to spin. I did this repeatedly and in different locations only to get the same results.

So, now, with my brother visiting, I asked him what he made of it. He had no answer. At that point, I had to take a quick leak. When I came back, I found my brother playing with the compass in different spots, observing the same results as I. For the record, my brother is a union carpenter. His specialty is drywall and metal studs. The house had only wooden beams. Shortly after that, he got on his scooter and drove off. I could only imagine what was going through his mind.

I decided to play things out a bit more. I called the landlord and left a message. I gave a brief description of the magnetic field in the ceiling. Two days later, he returned my call. I guess Fay had to tutor him.

Once into our conversation, he said, "What do you want me to do-- call Ghostbusters!?" I guess I just wanted to hear what asinine answer he would give me. How right I was.

As I pushed "end call" on my cell phone, I was thinking about what else would piss Fay off. I had a thought that would involve bringing a female into the picture. But would that be using good judgment on my own behalf and that of hers? That angle must have grabbed the devil's pitchfork because there was this tug of war on my shoulders. My mind couldn't make the proper decision. Besides that, I was too picky. So, for the time being, onto the back burner that went.

AT THE HUT

16

July 9th, 2009. My mind was dazed and my body felt like it was laced with kryptonite. I knew this day would come sooner or later, but it had come far too soon. My son, Zorro, had to be put down. The tears just rolled down my face like a dripping faucet. I wanted answers: "Why!?"

In a month's time, I had seen bumps multiplying on his skin. He had just turned seven years old on Father's Day. I took him to the vet to get a biopsy. I didn't know how to explain it to one of the girls working that morning. Zorro's veterinarian was in, so I proceeded to discuss with her my situation, telling her my house was triangulated. I gave her the police report so that she could make a copy. I was very forward and direct. I wanted any and every test to be done. I was determined. Thoughts of Fay's system were going through my mind-- images of an energy field coming from the cell tower. A magnetic field.

I knew that too much of anything, inside or outside your body, was unhealthy. Fay and their triangulated toy had been locked on my residence for over a year. From the research I did and inquiries I made, I was informed it was harmless, but my concerns remained. One regarded whether a test had ever been conducted on a dog in a triangulated field for an extended period of time. Usually, if someone is being triangulated or surveilled, it is for three months at the most, and with a subpoena. Not a fuckin' year, nonstop, as I was.

That evening, I picked my boy up. Earlier in the day, I had gotten him some real rawhide bones, not the generic ones that swell up in the stomach. I didn't cut any corners when it came to my son. When we got home, I made his dinner, but he didn't eat. I just thought he was delusional from the anesthesia and needed some time out-- time with his dad.

The following day, more bumps appeared, so I called the vet for an explanation. She told me she would prescribe an antibiotic called Cephalexin for his skin. I went to get his medication that morning. The vet instructed me to see how it worked. If it didn't, we would stick with Prednisone. As the weekend went by, I could tell my boy's ailment was getting the better of him. I called the vet again and went to pick up his Prednisone.

I rushed back home and popped two pills in Zorro's mouth. I whispered in his ear, "Be strong for Daddy." The following day, his hip movement was different, and not in a good way. I just saw how he looked at me. He was in pain. That evening, I put the massager on him, as well as ice. I was grasping at straws. I didn't want to face the reality that my boy would be leaving me.

The following morning, he really couldn't move. I got a big beach towel and put it under his 160-pound body. I hoisted him up and told him "Daddy gotta." He trusted me. We went outside to the car. I started the car up and proceeded to drive to Zorro's final destination. As I was driving, I had my rear view mirror tilted downward so I could see him lying down. Any other time, he would have had his head hanging out of the window with the wind blowing by his face. Not today.

We arrived at the vet. I walked inside. The one lady said, "Don't say anything, Paul." She could tell.

As she gave me a hug, I mumbled, "I tried everything."

"I know you did," she answered.

"I know you see this often with families."

"You and Zorro were different," she replied. "I know he was very special."

We went outside. They brought out a stretcher and, as we slid Zorro out of the car, he let out a yelp of pain. At that point I couldn't hold back. I broke down. I kissed his wet nose and said "You'll never be forgotten."

I asked to have him cremated. I passed the woman one of his favorite toys. I just left. I was bitter. I guess, at that point, I wanted to blame someone, but without proof, I couldn't go that route.

Afterward, I drove to Valley Forge Park and just sat there for hours. Finally, I said, "Okay. It's time to move on."

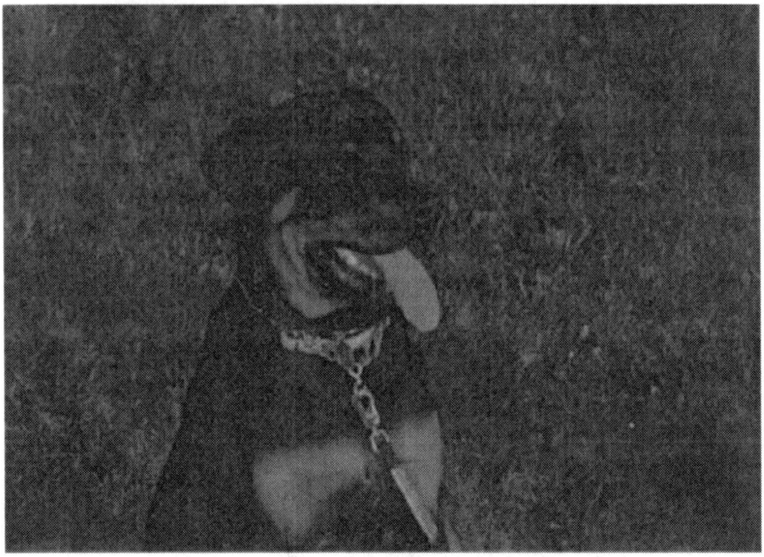

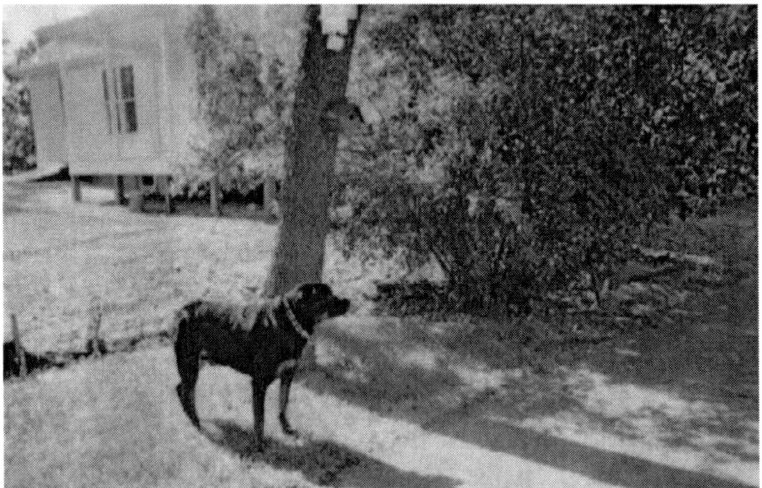

DIAGNOSTICS

Animal Hospital Client # 4912
                    Chart #

Accession No.	Doctor	Owner	Pet Name	Received
NYBA0373162		SWIST	ZORRO	06/26/2009

Species	Breed	Sex	Pet Age	Reported
Canine	Rottweiler	CM	7Y	06/27/2009 05:29 PM

Test Requested	Results	Reference Range	Units

Biopsy

Biopsy
Microscopic Description: One section of haired skin is examined. A regionally severe infiltrate of epithelioid macrophages and neutrophils expands the dermis and subcutis. These cells form sheets and distinct pyogranulomas, often centered around clear vacuoles. The center of the focus is necrotic. The surgical margins are clean.

Microscopic Findings: Severe pyogranulomatous dermatitis and cellulitis with necrosis - Haired skin, left dorsal shoulder.

Comment: Possible causes for this pattern of inflammation include bacteria, acid fast bacteria, or fungi. Special stains to look for infectious agents in the lesion could be done. To order special stains to look for infectious organisms, call Customer Service at _____ and order a Gram stain (number 666), an acid fast stain (number 687) and a GMS stain (number 685). Culture of remaining lesions may also be indicated. If confident rule-out of infection is achieved, a diagnosis of exclusion remains: sterile granuloma and pyogranuloma syndrome is a relatively uncommon condition in which dogs present with multiple foci of sterile granulomatous and pyogranulomatous dermatitis and cellulitis. Since treatment involves immunomodulation, rule-out of infectious agents should precede treatment for this condition.

Report Notes:
L DORSAL SHOULDER

Page 1   FINAL   06/27/2009 05:29 PM

17

I had this one friend whom I've known for many years. He knows I am a bit on the wild side. A couple of times, I went to his house, but he wasn't home. I didn't like that because if Fay got wind of it, he would put a hold on the situation like in the past. Finally, on the third try, I caught up to him. Usually he asked me what I'd been up to. I would reply, "It's deep, real deep." I didn't need to say any more. He knew it was a "Female." I just gave him that smirk. So I got right to the point. I said, "Look, I need to get some counter-surveillance equipment."

"Okay," he said. I knew what I needed. It couldn't be some kind of knockoff equipment.

The bottom line was that you just don't buy something thinking you'll reveal a transmitter. You have to understand low frequency and ultra high frequency. Low is between 1 MHz and 1.5 GHz and high is 100 MHz to 10.5 GHz; these two combine to prevent any gaps when testing. All devices emitting electromagnetic radiation cause some kind of deflection. In other words, turn off any televisions, radios, etc., unless you want to schitz yourself out.

The piece I had in my hand was very sensitive. It was sweet. Even government agencies use it. I told my boy to overnight it. I didn't want any days to lapse and allow Fay to get it and alter it. So he placed the order for that piece. I needed one more thing; I told him I wanted a camera, a Mini-Hunter. I explained to him how it worked. Any wireless camera within 300 feet, depending on the output of the video transmitter, would be hunted down by the Hunter.

The Hunter is a receiver. Its range is 900 MHz to 2.7 GHz. When I would plug an earbud into the video and audio "socket" -- for which it's not meant -- I, just tinkering around, came to understand the different bands and sounds.

Each band had its own ringtones; for example, one for 901, one for 902, etc. Some would increase in tone while others would decrease.

When the technology came into play, suggesting "cellular triangulation," certain bands would be needed to retrieve the required data.

If that is not understandable, imagine you have an instrument, like a piano, which has an array of keys. The piano is a receiver intercepting my fingers' transmissions. Touching each key produces a unique sound, and a song can be created from these sounds.

The same principle applies to cell phones. They have bands and frequencies that identify them-- without those two components, the cell is useless.

The next day, I stopped by my boy's workplace. I had the equipment delivered there just to be on the safe side. Unfortunately, only the Hunter came.

"Just my luck," I said to myself. I took the Hunter and went home. Tomorrow was another day.

That evening, I was planning how I was going to peruse each area. I thought about a transmitter or video of some kind. I knew Fay was monitoring me 24/7. I also knew he was very well-trained and experienced. This wasn't going to be a walk in the park for me just because I invested in some counter-surveillance. But, if you don't try, you'll never know.

The next afternoon, the other piece came. My boy gave me my package. I thanked him and he wished me luck.

I just turned my head and gave him a cross-eyed stare. "I'll be in touch."

Driving back home, I was thinking about Zorro. Did I do all I could for him? Did I put him in harm's way? I guess I'll never find out. Only the Man upstairs knows. Even though Zorro was gone, I couldn't do anything irrational. That was what Fay would want-- for me to go off the deep end so they could say "See!? Paulie is a wackjob!" As I pulled onto the driveway, I snapped out of those thoughts.

That evening, I started to play around with my new toys, but I had my son on my mind. I couldn't focus on the situation, so I was just tinkering with it. I was exhausted. It was probably around 10:30 PM. I lay down and my mind was still working. I knew there were devices nearby. I started to backtrack with my thinking. When the landlord was upstairs, something didn't add up. I felt this adrenaline in me that I used to have when my son and I were outside running R-6 cable.

I turned the lights in both rooms on and grabbed my new toy. I thoroughly read what was recommended regarding low and high frequencies. In this case, it was recommended I use low with an attachable antenna. I started to scan the ceiling. I picked a couple of spots I had in mind. I was right on the money; I got a positive hit. I approached this other area and was two for two. Then I did the whole ceiling, and one more was revealed. I repeated this three times to be sure. I switched to high frequency, but the LED light didn't flash. That made sense. I couldn't see Fay's devices, but I could see in the windows where the hits were. There were closets right above that area. I would do more tests. Living in the finished basement, I had access to the circuit breakers. I turned the power off on the apartment above me and grabbed my toy, repeating the spots again... and, again, they were positive. That told me they were running off a battery.

My mind was somewhat pleased. A couple of days before I had to put Zorro down, I went to the police station and arranged an appointment with the Chief. I really didn't know what I was going to say to him, but I wanted to keep my appointment scheduled for 10:00 AM, Monday the 13th. That morning, I did my routine and headed to the station. The little chubby guy was behind the glass as usual.

"Chief in?" I asked.

"Yes," he replied. "He'll be right out."

As he came out the door, the Chief asked, "What can I do for you, Mr. Swist?" I explained to him that I found three devices in the ceiling. Once again I offered to show him how and what I used. He didn't hesitate this time. He drove his own vehicle and another officer came right down. The chief had known Zorro and expressed his condolences. I thanked him. I had heard that he was also a dog person. I guess he could relate.

As I showed him the hits, he asked me to do other spots. I did, but there were no hits in those spots. He seemed more curious about my toy than the hits. He even wrote down the name of my toy's manufacturer. The meeting only lasted 15 minutes. The officer took the landlord's number again. He mentioned Zorro again and left. As the officers were leaving, it seemed the only thing he was interested in was my toy.

The following Friday, I headed back up to the station to get a police report, only to be informed one couldn't be provided because there was an ongoing investigation.

"What else is new?" I asked as I walked out those doors again.

As I am still triangulated, I have to wrap this story up for now. I have to say, Fay got a lot of good shots on me. Remember, I am only one person. Their triangulating system is advanced. I am sure they get their targets 99% of the time, but there's that 1% that will burn them.

18

I figured out what I did without using a computer. I may have asked a couple of people to look things up for me but, for the most part, I was using common sense. As time went on, I really saw a change in people. It was as if I had leprosy. Fay intimidated people with his badge. He must have looked at me like people stereotype Susan Boyle. They underestimated her. His analogy of me and what he assumed was that he got outwitted.

Now, follow this closely: A triangle has three points. In other words, the points are the cell towers. Fay had a variety of ways to get my cell phones. I mentioned some of the ways. Midway through the event I was pressed to find a different solution to get a clean cell. What I discovered was unique on Fay's behalf. Now that I had my toy, and, basically, the majority of fuses removed from the fuse box, I could go to my destination and activate my cell.

Wrong!

As I said, follow me closely. I tried two different counties and two different cell companies, T-Mobile and Verizon. And Fay got both of them. "Damn!" I said. Understand, I could have brought the cell home to check it, but that would have defeated the purpose. My residence was triangulated and how I figured it out was that once cell tower was nine-tenths of a mile from my residence. Its magnetic field only goes so far, and then another tower takes over. So, any time I enter with a hot cell near the 0.9-mile tower, it triggers and goes back to Fay. How did I figure that out? I already knew the area and the streets where the towers switch up. So, I simply turned on my tape recorder and then my cell phone a little bit before the switch of the towers takes place, and I just listen for that distinct sound-- basically, whether I got a ping. I could also tell by the signal strength. Why do you have all those bars? Because, if your cell is hot and someone is monitoring you, the system will drain it a little and then bring it back up. This occurs because they are zeroing in. It's always best to start your cell fresh by removing both the battery and the SIM card, if there is one. Now, you are ready to observe.

At this point, I was determined to defeat Fay. I had wasted money and days driving.

"Okay... let's see if you catch this one," I said. Once I drove to the King of Prussia Mall, I parked the car in one of the garages and walked to the bus stop to wait for a bus heading to Center City, Philadelphia. So far, so good. This time, I purchased a Cingular cell phone. The guy asked for my name, so I gave him a false one: Pete Hanley. I then asked him whether he had any prepays. He showed me a couple of them. I didn't like the ones with Bluetooth technology. Any cell phone with that accessory is bad, really bad. Your cell could be on standby or even turned off and _they can still listen in!_

If you plan on a deep, private conversation, take the cell phone battery out. That is a must. The rules of the game are: Don't make yourself paranoid. Watch what kind of counter-surveillance you buy, or you'll be chasing R-F signals like some kind of exotic butterfly. R-F signals surround us every day. And always trust your pet!

19

CDMA (Code Division Multiple Access) is a competing cell phone service technology to GSM.

GSM (Global System for Mobile communications) is the most popular system for mobile phones in the world.

TDMA (Time Division Multiple Access) is a cell phone technology that works by dividing each digital cellular channel into three time slots, increasing the amount of data carried.

TSCM (Technical Surveillance Counter-Measures) is the original United States Military abbreviation denoting the process of bug-sweeping.

R-6 CABLE is coaxial cable wherein all of the components are arranged about one axis.

RF is the initialism for radio frequency, defined as any frequency within the electromagnetic spectrum associated with radio waves. If RF current is sent to an antenna, an electromagnetic field which travels through space is created.

20

    Imagine yourself being videoed and listened to 24/7, and harassed on top of that. You try to get attorneys and law enforcement to help and then you come up empty-handed. I didn't mention that I discovered two video cameras inside the gym and also outside the gym on telephone poles. I didn't even bother to report it. Fay knew I was aware of them, but I couldn't touch them for legal reasons. They might come at me. Fay's system is very advanced. My house was a perfect setting for Fay to triangulate because of two vacant upstairs apartments and an unoccupied house next door.

    The one thing about which I remain very curious was my trip to Philadelphia, and just how they got that one cell. I know Sherman and Hunter Counties were given grants to purchase their triangulating systems, so that tells me there's a connection. It somehow must scan any new numbers being activated. Then they are programmed into their computerized technology.

    Anyway, I give my respects to the Chief. I didn't expect him to take my side. If I were in his shoes, I would do the same.

He might bend a little for his detectives, but he wouldn't twist something around. I also believe that, after Zorro passed away, a thought went through his mind that I could snap, and it would be ugly. That would not go over well if push came to shove.

When you consider all the time and money and countless hours poured into my situation, it makes your mind wander. In the month of July 2009, a young female in her teens was at a major outlet store in Lower Origin. She was stalked and sexually assaulted. A media conference was held with all the major news stations in attendance. What I am getting at is that someone is directing attention my way when it should be on the dude who attacked the woman.

I also wonder what was going through Fay's mind. There are two listening devices: one right above my bathroom and one in my bedroom. He didn't want any females around me. Is he sexually obsessed with me?

Finally, there's the landlord. He always liked when I paid him cash. That only tells me he's hiding his income. I think a government agency would be interested in his bookkeeping.

21

To whom it may concern:

I bring this letter and attached documents to you for many reasons. As I describe just some of the many incidents that have occurred after I submitted these documents to officers of the court, I hope you will see my dilemma. Ninety percent of my everyday routine has been altered or affected by law enforcement abusing their authority and using technology by means of my cell phone. As an example, I'll be talking with my mother in Florida, and, in the middle of the conversation, the phone is disconnected. It is off for an extended period of time (it is not just a dropped call) and then turned back on the next morning. This has occurred to me twice. Another example: Females I meet are approached and told I am under investigation. This occurs after the female sends me a text message. The message is intercepted. I honestly could not believe this was happening to me at first. So, over the months, I basically used two female friends to prove what was going on. Another incident happened when I went to visit a male friend at a local gym. A couple of days later, he informed me that I was not allowed in the gym any longer. When I asked why, his manager mentioned something about harassing a female. I responded "okay" and just laughed.

Please understand that this is just the tip of the iceberg. Since I submitted the attached documents, I have gone through about 30 prepaid cell phones. Am I under investigation or is this a vendetta against me? Understand this is no "Joe the Plumber" on his computer. This is law enforcement and their technology being used. I have kept a record and can tell you how they are using it, where, when, and who. I am simply at a loss as to what I can do to get justice for myself. I respect your decision if you choose not to get involved with this matter further, but I need someone who is willing to listen to the full story and is willing to be persistent.

22

To: Central Intelligence Agency
From: Paul Swist

To whom it may concern,

I bring this to your attention because I feel this is a security matter. As you read this, my residence has been under surveillance for 10 months or more by local law enforcement in Sherman County, PA. I tried numerous ways to resolve the matter, including calling the FBI. As I was talking with the agent on the phone, the call was interrupted. I have tried to contact a lawyer but my mail is tainted. Female friends are told I am under investigation. I even tried to bring this matter to the local Chief of Police at least four times. If this were the case, my house being "triangularized," they would have to have a subpoena. I know this is true, but someone is abusing this situation. I informed the Chief of Police about the surveillance system. I told him I basically figured out how many seconds it takes from the tower when it is on manual and automatic. I even mentioned to the Chief that the only day it was not on was the day before April 1st because of the computer virus. I offered to the Chief the opportunity, if he wanted, to come to my residence, and I would show him. I have no need or interest in the system. I have documentation to back this up. I ask you, don't just make that one call and hear one side of the story. Let me walk you through and hear my side... that is all I ask. You can then make your own decision. Thank you.

23

Dear Mr. Kuei,

I bring this information to you because of what you represent. It's one thing, me showing and demonstrating, versus me writing, but I will do my best. Anyway, without me going into too deep of detail, a cell phone booster and common sense tells it all. Its function is to take my signal to the cell tower. I use this device because of the way my residence is designed-- it's like a bunker. It works off 1850-1900 MHz *only* and it will not pick up any other signal unless it detects an unwanted signal, at which time it goes through a resetting procedure. My cell tower is 0.9 miles from my place, which is very good. So, the objective of triangulating a house is to pinpoint a cell or retrieve a signal frequency. This has been locked on for at least two years. Now comes the reason why I am contacting you. I had a seven-year-old Rottweiler, Zorro, to whom I was very, very attached. In one month's time, these bumps protruded on just his back-- as many as you can see in the report or imagine. The tower is 0.9 miles away and the RF signal is coming down at a force. You may ask yourself, "Do I know who it is?" It was Sherman County law enforcement that has this vendetta against me. As you may know, a dog's skin is completely genetically different from ours. The zars value varies in different devices; the most that is allowed is six. What I am trying to describe and say is that too much of anything in or out is not good for your body, meaning my dog, for such a period of time. They may have tested mice or a rat for a month. Well, I think you may understand what I'm stating. On December 28, 2009, I went over to my neighbors' house. They are two elderly people-- very nice. Long story short: When I was greeted at their door, I asked them whether they were having problems with their motion detector. They replied by saying that they had had an electrician and the builder look at it and neither could understand why it kept coming on at night. I then proceeded to explain. I apologize and here is another one for the devices that veer rodents always. They have sort of an electronic sound. But when the signal is torn up, there's a magnetic deflection, which makes it hum.

24

I put the majority of this story out in advance for a couple of reasons. My intention wasn't to write a book. Anyone who wants to publish a book won't pass out early copies to reveal the story. Yes, I did brag about it. I told my mother, brother, and sister, along with others I knew. But I also knew Fay was always listening in. By putting out my intent to write a book, I was aiming to get Fay's attention. As you read, I tried to get legal help. I was unsuccessful. So I thought, perhaps, I would print 10 copies of my story and hand them out to different individuals. Some I did out of kindness, to let them know what was going on in the neighborhood or at the gym. Others were given to people who I knew were Fay's confidential informants. I had a notion that, if Fay read it, perhaps they would veer away from me. Well, let me tell you, it didn't go over well. Fay was irritated... very irritated, I heard.

As an example of how I wanted to show kindness and concern, I passed on a copy to a neighbor living directly behind my residence. I told him that I would pick it up in a couple of days. Two days later, in the evening, I knocked on his door and the dude acted like a different person. He looked at me like I had leprosy, mentioning about his son having headaches due to the magnetic field from the triangulation. He also informed me that his son was scared of me. Just for the record, I never met his son. I wouldn't even recognize him if I ran into him. The dude also said to me that he couldn't understand why anyone would want to read a story like this. When I asked whether there was anything else he wanted to add, sarcastically, he said, "Good luck publishing it."

"Oookay!" This time, it was me walking away and shaking my head. When I returned home, I checked the papers he returned to me. There were four pages missing. "There're all kinds," I muttered to myself.

I believed I had to put some of my adventures from my late teens into the story because they were part of my "guy conversations" at the gym. To be sure, Fay knew all about those conversations. It was important to me to show that I was sincere. For many months, I knew what was up. I had to play it out by way of letting Fay and his stooges hear what I wanted them to hear, see what I wanted them to see, and finally read what I wanted them to read.

Another neighbor, right beside me, owns a house which has been vacant for a couple of years while being on the market. I knew Fay had the triangle on his property without his permission. There was no subpoena throughout this episode. One evening, I was out front with my cell phone booster and video camera. Fay thought I was up to my old tricks with the booster. When I went toward the dude's property with the cell booster in one hand and the video camera in the other, they figured out what I was actually doing. The next thing I knew, the cell phone booster wasn't flickering. I gathered up my stuff and waited for the right night. I knew there was a video transmitter out front, on the second floor of my residence, shooting down at the driveway. It would be well worth waiting for the right night by taking advantage of that situation in order to show Fay does whatever they choose.

Two days later, in the evening, at around 11 PM, it was cloudy and dark. I had to be quiet because of the listening devices on the first floor. I turned the TV up and strolled over to the neighbor's backyard, hooked up the booster, and the magic began to flicker. I stood there videoing it for about 15 to 20 minutes until I was satisfied I had my information. Then I ninja-ed myself over to my driveway and proceeded to video from that angle until I was again satisfied. When I finally caught up to the neighbor, I presented him with a copy of the story and also a video. I also apologized for going onto his property, but he was not offended. I started to elaborate on triangulation, omnidirectional antennae, and a geometric/mathematical standpoint. Then I saw his face. He didn't understand. I just referred him to the story and told him to watch the video.

I also found out that Fay changed my words to use them against me. For instance, when I was deep in conversation, I would say, "I swear on Zorro." That was, and still is, just my way of letting someone know I was sincere. But Fay would use that phrase as a reverse-psychology method when they would talk to people to persuade them against me. In other words, Fay made it sound as if I would swear on my own son.

Now, nearing the midpoint of my story, one of my deepest wishes is to be challenged by a technician to prove the reality of the episodes by playing my technology and countermeasures against Fay's.

I would like to think I am a normal person and not some kind of drug lord. When I think about my past and my first arrest... it was very bizarre. Long story short, I was driving down a motor highway and I saw lights flashing. Five dudes had their guns pointed my way.

"Someone must have just robbed a bank!" I said to myself. But when I looked in the mirror, there was nobody. Just me. At that point, I knew it was about Paulie. While I was sitting in the car, with all the guns pointed at me, I saw to my right, in a field, a helicopter landing. An older gentleman jumped out, holding his hat against the force of the twisting blades, a cigar hanging from his mouth. It was then that I knew who was approaching me, and he was saying, "Swisty, we gotcha... we gotcha."

My second arrest was <u>déjà vu</u> all over again. This time, I was in my boy's house. The house was all videoed up. I asked about some noise. The next thing I heard was lots of footsteps coming downstairs followed by "FBI! DEA! US Marshals!" I just sat there. My mind was numb.

As I said before, we choose our own destiny, whatever it may be. And no matter what, mine will haunt me to the end.

25

Another year has passed. Now, 1,095 days later, I am still triangulated and dealing with all the bullshit that follows it. After three years you'd think I would snap or go off the deep end. As I said in the beginning, I believe in respect. I am only one person. My life is not normal, *by no means.* No mortal person could live his days the way I do. You have to believe in yourself and for what you stand. I know the Man upstairs watches over me. I don't go to church, but He knows I am a true believer. I'm not afraid to die. I can honestly say that. He knows that, too. If the time comes for me to leave (this world), I hope it's for saving a life... that of a child.

Millions have been spent and a ton of man-hours invested. My body is surrounded by RF signals. My name should be Radio Frequency instead of Paul Swist. I realize that this is not going to end any time soon. So, let it be. Since May 2009, I have looked back at the tactics directed at me. Both humorous and sad events play through my mind every single day. I think about him all the time... till this very day. (I can't speak his name.) I never retrieved his ashes. I couldn't go back to the vet. My inner self grieves over what happened to him. You may not understand unless you are a true dog person. I can only imagine what a parent feels when losing a son or daughter. The saying is, "Time heals." I don't believe that. It has to linger in the mind. But, in the end, I suppose everybody deals with their situations as best as they can, just as I am.

Yes, what I'm going through is out of the ordinary. Throughout my life, things just happened to me. This ordeal is extremely out of the ordinary... like the time I got my first toy, the one that went from 1 MHz to 10 GHz. It was August 2009. I drove to a parking lot a few miles away from my place. It was a hot, humid day. I was frustrated. I still didn't quite understand my toy when it came to using it to uncover a GPS transmitter, if there really was one in my car. I was sitting on the edge of a curb and I looked up to the sky like I was talking to God.

"Give me a break," I said.

All of a sudden, around eight geese, in formation about 200 yards up, appeared. The next thing I knew, a pile of shit hit my right shoulder and the right front fender of my car. I looked up again, not worried about wiping it off my shoulder, and I asked, "Is that where it is?" The geese were trying to tell me that the "Eye in the Sky" was the way Fay was tracking me. Shaking my head, I said, "Only me would this happen to!" Long story short, I didn't find a transmitter.

Back in the beginning of this, when I hired the dude from NJ to check my car out for a hidden GPS unit, I was on to Fay. He just couldn't accept it. If I knew then what I know now about receivers, I could have really put the dude on the spot. I now know when I am coming within 75 yards of my residence. My receiver signals let me know. I also knew damn well that he was picking signals up. He even told me he drove up and down the street. The bottom line was that the dude from New Jersey took my money like a true scumbag!

Here's an example of another thing I didn't, at first, understand. I didn't understand why or how it was occurring. In a year's time, I went through three car batteries. Finally, after the third one, I understood. The electricity surrounding my car had drained my battery. It wasn't that I had a bad alternator or that anything mechanical was wrong. Each time I took the batteries back to the auto place, they tested them and informed me that the charge was lost. I just laughed to myself. How did I fix the problem? I disconnected the battery every time I came home.

Another time, I heard about this spy shop in Philadelphia. I had plans to meet up with a female on South Street, so I got down there early. I took a bus from King of Prussia. As I was walking, I asked this dude if he knew where the *Spy Shop* was located. He directed me two blocks down and to the right.

"Cool," I said, "I don't have far to walk." I thanked him. Well, the next thing I knew, I was looking up and reading the words *Spice Shop.* *Idiot!* I thought. *How could he not hae understood what I said?* I had to backtrack and continue down South Street again. Then I saw a T-Mobile phone store and thought *They've got to know.* Inside were two dudes, the owner and a worker.

"Excuse me," I said. "Do you know where the **SPY Shop** is?"

They looked at each other. Finally, one dude said, "Yeah, three blocks down on your right-hand side. A little Korean guy owns the place." As I left their store, I thought, *It's about time.* Well, wouldn't you know it? I looked up at the sign and it read "**SPA Shop.**" I went inside thinking that maybe they carried spy equipment, too. A little Korean man greeted me by asking if I wanted a girl.

"No!" I replied emphatically. When I asked him for the **SPY Shop,** he told me that was the **SPA Shop.** I just shook my head. Then he asked me if I was gay.

"This can't be happening."

26

    I've gotten more experience with Fay's technology than you can imagine. You might even say I'm addicted. It may be hard for you to relate to how I can be so involved with counter-surveillance, but if you look back to how I started to understand my experience, you'd realize it stems back to a $15 tape recorder. It's a lot like Sherlock Holmes. He started with a $5 magnifying glass. I took it to the 21st century with a cheap tape recorder-- not even a digital one. That's all I had. No computer. No help. Just common sense and me. Fay's equipment and technology are state-of-the-art. You don't get any better than that! But now, here I am, shining like a brand new copper penny right out of the mint!
    Unfortunately for Fay, if he hadn't played around with texting me, interfering with females and all of his other unprofessional bullshit, I wouldn't have figured out Fay's surveillance technology. They were stunned by what I used and how I used it. On the other hand, they learned a lot from my counter-surveillance. They knew only fifty percent. They didn't

know how I had my stuff set up. They couldn't have. Let me tell you why.

There was a period of six months in 2009 during which the elderly couple living in a house next door to me -- the nicest people you could meet, by the way -- became aware of what was going on. They saw it with their own eyes and experienced it through problems with two motion detectors installed on either side of their house. Their property connects with mine via a driveway that separates both houses. During that six-month period, one of their motion-detecting lights was set off for no apparent reason, staying on for most of the day, even in daylight. They had their building contractor look at the motion detector. He couldn't figure it out. An electrician was hired to look at it. He didn't know either. No one did until I came over and explained what was occurring.

When Fay was trying to get the frequency signal to line up, it was happening. Their system-emitted electricity was causing a deflection. Every time they tried to adjust it, the motion detector was tripped. To top that, someone disconnected the rear motion detector, disabling it. By pointing that sensor downward, there was no deflection. When I was explaining the problem to the couple, they informed me that their house alarm was also going off. The same principle applied here as with the motion detectors. The lady told me she went to the Township but got nowhere with her complaint.

"They could at least pay for the electric!" she said with a sense of humor. I apologized to her again. "You should do your own reality show, Paulie."

From time to time I would chitchat with the couple. She observed that, when I left my house, there often were cars sitting in my driveway or out front by the curb. I explained once again what they were trying to achieve. It all revolved around the cellular signal. Fay sent one of his stooges out to my house. As they sat in or along the drive, talking on a cell phone, the signal was angled upward.

All throughout my experience, which is going into its third year, you could not imagine how many countless times dudes and females pulled into the driveway. I am talking about all the way into the back, behind my house! There was and still is no excuse. When I questioned them, they told me that they were interested in renting one of the apartments. For the last two years, you couldn't make out a telephone number on the "For Rent" sign. I let it be known that it is only common sense that, if you're renting an apartment, you're going to make sure the phone number can be read. Soon after, Mr. Wilson, the "landlord," put his landline and cell numbers on the sign.

He was a true slumlord, but I played him just like the rest, needless to say. Good old Mr. Wilson. He was working for Fay. It was a joke. I truly think he thought he was some kind of James Bond character. At least 10 times in my recall, Mr. Wilson was lining up the signal. I knew the boundaries of the signal. One time, in order to direct the left-side signal, Mr. Wilson was at the edge of the driveway, talking on his cell phone. I was parallel to him about 15 yards away. I knew Fay could see me by way of a video camera on the telephone pole across the street. Mr. Wilson moved in a little closer and onto the driveway. Shaking my head, I, too, moved closer. Here's the reason he was doing this: If the frequency signal is too close to the street, Fay's system will pick up any car that has a cell phone in use and will try to correct the signal angle using the wrong data. That motion detector going off and on was embarrassing.

It was soon after this event that I noticed Fay had upgraded his technology. I asked myself, "How much better can he get?" I had to make a power move. I knew what I needed, but it was way out of my price range. There was a flea market that sold electronics. I would check the place from time to time. You never know what you'll find at those places. Maybe, one time, you'll buy an old picture, and then decide you want to put it into a new frame. You discover a hidden copy of the Declaration of Independence. You just never know! Well, this one time, I went and found it staring right at me. I knew I was looking at a 1 MHz-6 GHz Frequency Finder!

Let me expand your mind so you'll understand. My latest toy has a strength meter that detects the electromagnetic field radiating from a transmitter. It has no means of screening or selecting frequencies. But, on the other hand, it still works well; you just have to be careful of false readings. That takes practice. Other means include broadband receivers and audio feedback. These receivers do not require intensive training. Audio feedback receivers rely on an amplifier to enhance a room's audio. When sweeping near a hidden device, if it turns up a transmitter bug, it will produce a loud squeal. Again, it's just okay. Another has tuning capabilities. A tuning receiver will provide more analysis of the area. The more elite and sophisticated receivers are spectrum analyzers and non-linear junction detectors (NLJDs) used by more serious counter-surveillance people. The ultimate way to go is thermal imaging. This works off of heat. Any bug transmitter, even a tape recorder that doesn't produce any frequencies -- just heat from the little motor inside -- will give a thermal reading. This device is so sensitive that, if I walk on your carpet an hour before you come home, the thermal imager would pick up my footsteps. This device is not cheap.

So, as Fay and his stooges came at me with all of their technology, I picked up on something out of the ordinary. At the time, I didn't understand what it was, but I did know why, and later, how. What tipped me off was a kind of antenna draping from the unit Fay used and the locations where they were placed.

From my house, there are four exits onto the main streets. Three of these frequency receivers were placed on telephone poles with street lighting. The objective of this device is to retrieve your cell phone number. If you stop below the spiral antenna with your cell phone on, your frequency signal will go up to the antenna, into the unit, and then onto Fay's system, where it is modulated to grab your phone number. At two of the exits, there weren't any because there wasn't a telephone pole conveniently placed, so a unit couldn't be installed to collect signals. I counted about 30 of them in my area, with a couple of stray ones in other townships I frequented. To top it off, all of those I noticed were hanging from lights, except for one (and only one), on my street, about a block down from the house. It had a special pole put there with the spiral unit dangling from it. I also noticed that some of these units had camera lenses. This caused me to drive through many townships to look for something similar. I discovered one other township that had a few, and I believe that they had the technology first. Fay later decided that he could possibly benefit, and then he directed his nefarious scheme at me. It turned out to be worthless, probably costing another $500,000. Now, I am sure that they could use his technology on other individuals, but if you look at the time frame when they were installed and positioned, it doesn't take a cavedude to figure it out.

My new toy was almost perfect, but I knew what else was needed in this era of technology: a range of antennae to use with different signals. The stock antenna was only good for digital/analog signals. I went to Radio Shack and purchased another antenna. It worked great. I was happy when I used it outside. I could even tune my receiver on unwanted signals. Now I was seeing unusual flashes in the bars going across every 15 seconds. The signals were on the same side as the landlord's and Fay's stooges. When I went to the back part of the basement, I got the same readings, time in, time out. It was consistent; I even videoed them.

"What's next?" I asked myself. Fay was pissed. I guess he felt he got punked three years in a row. Everybody was talking about him, including his peers.

27

The next thing with which I dealt was the landlord showing the second-floor apartment to this dude. He was a white male, five-foot-eight, and about 160 pounds. The landlord informed me that he was an optician.
"You have a renter, finally," I said to Mr. Wilson. He also informed me that the dude was going through a separation. I replied "Okay" and walked away, rolling my eyes. One day, I saw the dude get out of his vehicle with a Radio Shack bag in his hand, along with a lamp. That was bold of Fay. He knew I was aware of what was actually going on. The dude was a technician. Over time, I observed him coming home in the morning and running upstairs. Two minutes later, he was out on the driveway and in his car. At night, around 9 PM, he returned, staying until about eleven. There were times when he would leave and return one half-hour later... probably for the following reason.
I played with him. One day, last winter, after a deep snow, I shoveled only the one driveway. I left all the snow on the other side where Fay always pulled in. I also left snow on the steps

leading to the second-floor apartment. There was no need for me to shovel the snow, but the whole concept of this plan was to see any kind of tracks... to play it out. One day, I came home from the gym and saw footprints, maybe size 8, leading up the steps. There wasn't much I could do about it, but it gave me satisfaction.

I would run R-6 cable out to the street and against the curb. I knew the boundaries where I could get a safe signal out. As I have said before, they were somewhat aware of how I was doing this. One day, Mr. Wilson was in the first-floor apartment, right above the location of my 13-inch TV. It always busted up their shit. Mr. Wilson was in the room above my TV for about three hours. My equipment picked up the frequent pinging of his cell phone. My new toy was so good that, if there was a cell phone within 25 feet of the receiver, I was going to know of its presence by the pinging sounds. Let me remind you again that it's about zeroing in on the signal. Sometimes I would play along. Other times I would let them chase after butterfly signals to show-and-tell how I was 200% right. Obviously, that day didn't go well for the technician.

About a week later, Mr. Wilson notified me that the heater guy was coming over. I said "Okay." I knew what was going through his mind and what was up. But, in fact, the heater hadn't been working properly, or it had broken down. A few days later, Mr. Wilson arrived with the heater guy. When I opened the door, I told them that they would have to leave their cell phones outside or in their vehicles.

"Why?" Mr. Wilson asked. Because of the frustrated look he gave me, I gave the lame excuse that my girlfriend was a nurse and she kept sensitive medical equipment there. Their phones could cause interference. "What if I miss an important phone call?" I gave him a penetrating stare. Afterward, they both put their cells away and then came in. I watched Mr. Wilson. I understood his body language. He was looking for R-6 cable wires. Mr. Wilson thought that I had sabotaged his heater. The guy with him was there to give a second opinion about the heater. The guy didn't even test for carbon monoxide, a test that is required.

Mr. Wilson's only interest was in seeing whether anything had been tampered with. Next thing I know, Mr. Wilson is looking at my 13-inch TV. It wasn't on, but he was staring at it as if it were some exotic stripper. He told me I had to take it down because there was a one-half-inch hairline crack in the ceiling.

Now you're pressing your fucking luck, I thought. He knew it. While the heater guy was still observing the furnace, Mr. Wilson was looking at the rear part of the basement. I noticed he had a Friendly Environment stick-um, about four inches by eight, stuck to his sneaker. When I told him, he looked down at it.

"It could have been Friendly Environment toilet paper instead," I said. He climbed the steps, mumbling something. As I watched Mr. Wilson trying to gather input on any wiring, I saw a Friendly Environment stick-um on his other sneaker. I busted up laughing and pointed at it.

"Get it off me, Paulie!" he exclaimed. He bent his leg up. I tried pulling it off, but only the part that wasn't stuck to the sole came free.

"Look at the bright side, Mr. Wilson," I said. "The bottom will last longer." As he left my apartment, I muttered after him, "That's what the fuck you get for being a James Bond wannabe."

Finally, the technician moved in, but I didn't exchange small talk with him. I also wasn't going to say "I know what you're doing." What I did do was wait for him. One evening, I was conveniently outside with my receiver. When he got out of his vehicle and walked to the steps, I crossed his path, saying, "Look at this."

"What is it?" he replied. I told him it was a receiver that detects video and audio signals. He knew damn well what it was.

I continued the conversation by saying "Look, Teddy, when I raise it up toward the apartment, the bars start to go across the receiver."

"Damn!" he exclaimed.

"Knowing you're going through a divorce," I continued, "I wonder whether your wife had a listening or video device planted up there. Or, Mr. Wilson could be a pervert and is watching you." As Teddy was thinking of how to reply, I added, "I could do a sweep of your apartment."

"Maybe another time."

We both laughed and parted to go to our respective apartments, with me remembering how I gave him the name Teddy.

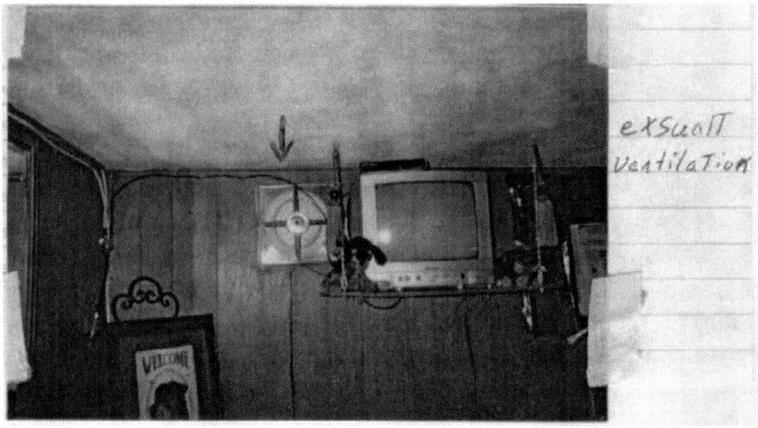
exsualT
ventilation

28

One day, when I arrived home, there was a Verizon van in the same old driveway. I asked the dude, "What's up?" He replied that he had to hook up Teddy's phone line. I knew his real name. I guess that was the name he used on previous investigations.

Fay was desperate. Remember that there was over a million dollars invested in me over the years-- with nothing to show for it. It's been the same old pattern. Remember my probation officer? You have to understand I was sentenced to eight years, supervised in my last five months. My probation officer sent me a certified letter stating he wanted me to come to his office. I knew something was up, and it wasn't early release of probation. He informed me of his concerns regarding my "mental health issues." In the past, any time he came over to my residence, I never mentioned anything about listening devices of any kind.

At the Federal Court House, on the day of my probation hearing, the judge was pissed. He leaned over his desk and asked the probation officer, "Don't you have better things to do? Why did you call Mr. Swist's girlfriend twice on her birthday at 9 AM?" The probation officer just stuttered. The judge sat back in his chair, took off his glasses, and said, "As of now, Paul Swist, your probation is terminated."

"Thank you, Your Honor," I replied. I packed up my papers, put them in my Nike shoebox, and went over to shake hands with the prosecutor and the probation officer. I just gave them a quick look but kept my mouth shut.

The probation officer didn't give a flying fuck about my well-being. Don't you think it would raise a red flag in the mind of a federal judge if someone were to state that there were satellites orbiting his house? When you read the letter that was addressed to the judge, you can see it was "scripted" by Fay! If you look at the police report I filed regarding my residence being triangulated, know that I had stated nothing about orbital satellites. To top it off, I never received a report about listening devices. Where did the probation officer get that information?

Fay!

29

As I write this, it's been about ten months since the Police Chief was at my residence with the other officer. Once again, I went up to make an appointment with the Chief. This time it was to be about the letter that went to the federal judge-- and, also, to get a copy of the police report. I informed him that someone had falsified and altered a report. I also told him that I've known the officer who took the initial report for 30 years. He's a good man and an honest officer. He would not lie for me or for the Chief. The Chief agreed. At this time, I also showed him a video of the technician coming and going, including what he was driving, and a video (using my new toy) showing 15-second intermittent flashing signals. I continued to elaborate on issues ranging from my neighbors' knowing to Zorro's lab reports. I told him I didn't believe all those people had reason to lie to me. I spoke of enduring three years of bullshit. I want anyone who chooses to read this story to know that I truly believe in the Chief. Even with this happening in his township, I can honestly say that he is a good man. I know he finds me very interesting and probably the most unusual person he has ever met.

Using my words, I want to prove my respect for the Chief and for his detectives. I want to pass on information about the newest era in technology. While our economy is in a recession and criminals are on the prowl, more villains or saints could be questioned at the police station through the use of thermal imagery. Thermal imagery can be used like a polygraph to test and see who is lying and who is telling the truth. The difference between the two is this: The polygraph works off of the nervous system, while thermal imagery works off of body temperature. Normal body temperature fluctuates slightly above and below the norm of 98.6 degrees Fahrenheit. Like a polygraph, it would require consent, a set time for testing, and, of course, manpower. That costs money, but the main benefit is that even a cold-blooded killer can't regulate his body temperature.

During an interrogation, the detective would relax the individual just as a polygraph technician would do by asking obvious questions with mutually-known answers. In a thermal reading, there would be "hot spots." That's what the detective would need to focus on. An operator behind a one-way mirror observes the receiver and can see the hot spots elevating or returning to baseline as the detective asks questions.

Now, you may say that this may be a violation of someone's constitutional rights, because they can't see it and therefore aren't aware of it. If that's the case, all of those cell phone frequencies over the years coming onto the property and in the neighborhood where I lived should have been recognized as a violation of those rights. I and everyone else should have been notified that cell phones were being scanned. There had to be thousands because they never could line up the signal correctly. Surely that falls under the Privacy Act. Fay would be jammed up with paperwork for the rest of his life. But his mind works on the belief that what the people don't know won't hurt them.

It's a different story with regard to those frequency receivers that decorate light posts. When driving on a public street, you basically give up your rights. It's just like a video camera on a street corner; there's nothing you can do about them. Even if Mr. Wilson had given Fay permission to do his so-called "investigation" in my apartment, it still doesn't justify an invasion of my privacy. In my understanding of the Privacy Act, each and every person should be notified that his or her phone was being scanned. You could bet that Fay checked each and every cell phone frequency to see whether it was mine.

    When you consider all of the money invested, it would not justify this witch hunt. This electronic surveillance to which Fay has access is our government at its finest. The frequency receivers hanging from the telephone and light poles are useless. Now, the only thing I could see them as being good for is around Christmastime, when decorations are put up. You could hang a Christmas bulb on the spiral antenna.

30

You cannot defeat what's not made to be defeated. That means the "cell phone booster" most of all. I noticed Fay's tactic of trying to back his stooges' system off. If it was down too much, it would not serve any purpose. When his system was turned up, the booster would identify an unwanted signal. The technician tried different software to trick the booster, but I revealed that, too. I have all of this and more, but I can't go into Fay's mind. That's between him and the Man upstairs.

Through the grapevine, I heard that Mia got himself a cell phone booster. I guess Teddy and he were trying different methods and software to defeat it. The bottom line is that it can't be defeated. If the average Joe the Plumber would take the time to understand the flasher upon plugging one into an outlet, it would be so easy for the human eye to recognize the flashes of the lights.

Here is a way to top some of Fay's technology using the booster. Let's say you think there is a sophisticated GPA device on your car. You need to take it to a location other than your residence. Make sure the place you choose has a power source.

Also, *you do not want any cell phones to be on or around you.* Stretch an R-6 cable out upon the ground for about 25 feet. Attach the antenna to something around six feet high. Drive the car around for a couple of miles, just in case it may be a sleeper or motion-activated. Stop the car where you set up. Put the booster on the roof, plug it in, and watch the lights. You're looking for even just one out-of-the-ordinary flash. You must understand that *it won't pinpoint the GPS device.* For that you may need a receiver to lock on to the location of the device.

If you take the time to understand what I am saying by using common sense and out-of-the-ordinary means, you will be able to see a pattern with Fay and his broken-down technology. I didn't write down a lot of the immature bullshit, including how he interfered with my finances and how I am representing myself in the courts against the landlord. Fay could not control his bitterness and anger. His technology was his pride and joy. It wasn't just about me understanding Fay's surveillance, but about my understanding of what it represented... for good, and not for evil. I didn't need the cell phone booster or my other surveillance receivers to understand that. I had it down to a science. If you look up the definition of science, you learn that it means the observation of a study subject, the collection of facts, the reporting of results, *and* the use of methods that can be repeated "even in a courtroom."

If I were to demonstrate all of Fay's tactics and immoral thinking, it would make you wonder. With him, it's the same pattern, same bullshit. I've just gotten more aware. Three years is a long time to be under surveillance and triangulated. It goes beyond me. If you carefully read this, you can see how it all connects, how there is a pattern. For all that has gone into this you would think that I was Al Capone. But look at it this way: Fay feels he got "punked." Not one, not two, but three years in a row, his surveillance technology and tactics have been defeated. Let me again state that I wouldn't have figured any of this out if he hadn't played immature, bullshit games. I didn't write down some of the things he'd done because they were idiotic. It's like a six-year-old child with a toy; if someone takes it away and breaks it, the child cries. That's natural. But Fay's an adult. He can't accept that I busted his shit up. It's useless! Much like a credit card, if it gets stolen and used, you're going to cancel it. The card becomes useless. It's the same scenario.

The oil spill in the Gulf of Mexico remains big news as I am writing this. There are similarities between the oil company and Fay. The company is greedy. Fay suffers from pride. The Man upstairs does not tolerate either. The company has to deal with the media and Fay has to deal with higher-ups and must justify the huge amount of money spent with nothing to show for it. At least the company will eventually slow the oil leak within two or three months. Fay used up millions of dollars of technology over three years and, now, it's worthless. Sure, it could be of use on some crack dealer, but the more sophisticated person will be aware of how to defeat Fay's technology.

Not only did Fay use technology on me, but he also used it to fulfill his male fantasies. I am referring to his wife. He knew she was a single mom with a child and that she was looking for a job. He cock-blocked any other male from hitting on her. In other words, once Fay had any personal information on an individual, he started doing his thing. Once he grabbed the EMI number or cell phone frequency, he could basically do whatever he wanted. Let's say a dude sent a text message to her. Fay could intercept it. It's the same thing with calls. I'll bet you that, if she looked back on how they met, she would see that Fay had actually stalked her. To me, that's just pathetic behavior in a man. One thing that still bothers me was that I did not understand at first that there was a pattern with the females. Maybe he wanted me to bang his wife. Shit! All he had to do was drop her off. I would have even videoed it for him.

Now, Fay may feel that I've punked him over a three-year period and on at least 30 occasions. I would like to take credit for that... but I can't. Why? He punked himself. You may be asking how a man punks himself, and it's a good question. His behavior answers it. Me? I just use common sense and look for anything that's out of the ordinary. That's it. Fay is like the kid who cried wolf when there was no wolf. If someone keeps going at you, then you'll see the same old pattern.

Look, I'm just the writer, the voice of this story. Fay has been in law enforcement for over 20 years and has achieved many awards. He is a person who is recognized among his peers. For that, he should be inducted into <u>The Guinness Book of World Records</u> for the most years being punked, the most consecutive times being punked, and given a punked poor-sportsman award. I don't know if that's anything of which he should be proud;

although, if his record needs to be confirmed, and Guinness wants to have a sit-down with me to go through each one, I'll do it for Fay. It's not like I'm an asshole!

31

October 22nd, 2010. Time to move out of "the Hut," but not before making my statements. I have numerous court appearances-- district and county. They consisted of escrow, arbitration, and appeals. Many people said "Just move, Paulie." I said "It's not about that."

But the truth? For me to be making my argument in the courtrooms, I had to stay at the Hut. For the reason of putting Mr. Wilson on the spot.

The house is old. The wiring is rigged up such that part of the electricity on the first floor is connected to my own. I have no exhaust fan for my cooking stove; I know that's a safety hazard and a code violation. That's one of my tickets into the courts.

As we wear on, back and forth, in the different court proceedings, Fay's mind is distraught. He can't understand how I'm up his ass repeatedly.

As I am preparing to move, my brother stops by. I can tell that he's not comfortable being here, but I understand. So he begins to tell me that an FBI agent called and informed him that a

Nigerian man had my driver's license in his possession. At this moment, I know something is out of the ordinary.

I interrupt my brother, still talking. I say that, first of all, the address on the license is listed as my own. Second: At that time, I was still on federal probation. Now, common sense comes to my mind and dictates that, with today's climate of terrorism, one would think that I would be questioned by an agent, or my probation officer would inform me... and not my brother.

He then shows me the agent's telephone number. I say, then, to think about how all this sounds, on top of all the other bullshit. But my brother says he sounded legit. He asks me if I lost my license.

"No," I say, "not really. I always keep it up in my visor in the car." I explain that I don't check to see whether it's there every time I get in my car... but, this one time, I needed it, and it was missing, so I got a new one.

I start to tell my brother of Fay's tactics, but it's too deep for him to understand.

Fay put together another flop. He thought my brother would give the agent my cell number and that it would be passed on to him. Now, the common sense thing to do is, if you find somebody's license, you put it in the mailbox, and, on top of that, I never heard a damn thing about my driver's license.

When my court dates arrive (each one is different, but each revolves around my living conditions), they're no walks in the park. Mr. Wilson has a high-profile lawyer. And me? I have *pro se* representation, which means that I am representing myself. I had tried to hire a couple of lawyers, but they fell through.

"Whatever," I say to myself. "So let it be."

Fay knows on what I'm concentrating. At the end of 2008, I had gone to the Township Code Enforcement and met with the manager. He was the person who informed me what had to be updated. I began to deliberate on the issues soon after we set a time and a date for him to stop by. I shook his hand and thanked him.

I am walking out of the Code Enforcement doors. Right below is the Police Department. Little did I know how many times I'd be walking through those doors.

32

    My first court outing with Mr. Wilson was at the district courthouse. I wanted to start this issue so that the other proceedings could follow. I put some thought into this, as my mind was working! It dawned on me -- when I say "dawn," I mean "dawn." That's when the bats used to come out. There was a colony of them above my steps. The roof had a crack and the bat droppings were at the entrance to my apartment. Now, if you know the anatomy of a bat, you know that they eat at least double their weight every day. Before any bullshit started with Fay, I brought this matter to Mr. Wilson's attention, and he replied to me that, if he were to get rid of the bats, what would be left to kill the mosquitoes? So I cleaned it up myself. The following year, the bats returned. That time, I withheld my rent. Now, understand that it was during this timeframe when Fay came into the picture. By withholding my rent and sending Mr. Wilson a certified letter about the bat issues, I was forcing Mr. Wilson to take me to court.
    He wanted his rent money, and I just wanted to drag his ass in and out of the courts, to wear him down.

The day of that hearing, the judge was fair. Mr. Wilson didn't show up with his lawyer. Every once in a while, I would do the "whisper thing." I've told many people about the video and the devices above my ceiling on the first-floor apartment. Fay thought I was going to bring that up at that hearing. Why? Because I led him to believe that, in reality, I was going to stick to the bat issue.

I understand Mr. Wilson's character. He tries to bullshit and bully people. I was just setting him up for my own purposes. The wiring to my apartment would cost big money. So, after I tell the judge about the bat droppings, and how Mr. Wilson commented in reacted to my complaint, the judge asked to see the certified letter I'd sent and the date on it. That brought a smirk to my face. Now, Mr. Wilson's turn-- I could tell he was frustrated, but I let him bury himself with his own words... and that he did. He went on to the subject of Zorro. When I heard my boy's name, I zeroed in on his voice and what he said, and he made a comment that, when he goes to the bathroom, he shits five pounds. I left it alone, but he continued to say that when he cuts the grass--

The judge interrupted Mr. Wilson and I didn't want to hear another thing about the Rottweiler. It was just two months before that I had to put my son to rest. I looked over to my left with an expression of "You are a piece of shit liar." Mr. Wilson had a landscaper cut the grass. I then stood up and showed the judge a copy of what was required by the code enforcement with the electrical issues. I just wanted to be sure it was entered and documented into the court record. That was my objective-- not the fucking bats. Mr. Wilson was getting flustered; I could see it and hear his tone. Then, he mentioned to the judge that he had wanted to turn off my utilities. The judge stated to him provisions of the law that made such an act illegal. Mr. Wilson was nothing if not persistent. He said that, since he was the landlord, it was his property. Again, the judge stated that Mr. Wilson could not have followed through with his plan. The final outcome was that I was ordered to pay my rent to the county courthouse.

And Mr. Wilson had 10 days to get rid of the bats.

33

From there on out, any hearings would be conducted at the county courthouse. I had to educate myself on landlord-tenant law once or twice a week. I would go to the law library at the courthouse and read case laws, how to prepare motions, etc. I also went to different law firms and asked questions about landlord-tenant law. One time, I went to an upscale firm and met with a gentleman who was a bit familiar with my case and situation. I had let him read part of this story in the past.

Soon after the hearing with Mr. Wilson, his lawyer started to send me certified letters. It was going to be a battle and I wasn't going to back down.

So, as the gentleman greeted me with a handshake, I got right to the point and asked him if he would represent me on my appeal. He agreed to do so and cited a $2,500 retainer fee. I was hesitant, but I wanted to be optimistic about bringing him into this ordeal. I kept that thought in mind. About a month and a half went by and I had another hearing. I said to myself that the process was becoming too hectic.

Fuck this, I thought. *I need someone who's not going to sell me out.*

So I headed back to that firm. I was greeted by the secretary again. I knew in my mind that she was a good person. Plus, she also read part of this story, and knew it was dirty.

Regarding my attorney, I asked the secretary, "Is he a pit bull? Is he the one I want?" She nodded her head and replied in the affirmative. I trusted her. She knew I was out to take someone's head off. I guess there was a particular look in my eyes. She asked me what day would be good for a meeting.

"The sooner the better." It was scheduled for the next day.

That day, I returned to the firm with my $2,500. When the lawyer and I came face-to-face, I didn't offer to shake his hand, and vice versa. I just got right to the point. I said that I wanted him to understand. I just wanted him to do my appeal and I asked only that he understand what I was all about. I signed the contract and we went over a few details. I stood up, gave him a firm handshake, and said "Thank you."

"You're in for a world of an awakening, Mr. Wilson," I said to myself as I walked out those doors.

A week later, I got a letter from my new attorney stating that he would be unable to represent me. I went back to the firm. You can only imagine what was going through my mind. I was furious, but in another way, I was not. As we met in the lobby, my eyes had a slight squint to them. He saw it, and he knew.

He started to explain. "Paul, take this money and move."

"I said in our previous conversations that it's not about winning any kind of money," I replied. "It's about seeing and hearing the lies of others when I'm questioned under oath. Do you want more money?"

"It's not that, Paul." I guess he knew I was no quitter and I wasn't ready to move yet. He had his secretary prepare my appeal for me and he gave me case laws to support it.

"I envy you, Paul," he said at the end of our conversation, "for what you believe in."

"When I go into a courtroom," I said, "I know I'm going to break a grown man down." I shook his hand and gathered all my paperwork. The secretary had even organized my documents and put them in a big, brown folder. There must have been 80 pages or so.

She saw my eyes as I was opening the door. There was fire in them and it wasn't directed at her or my attorney.

That's when I finally came to the conclusion that I was on my own.

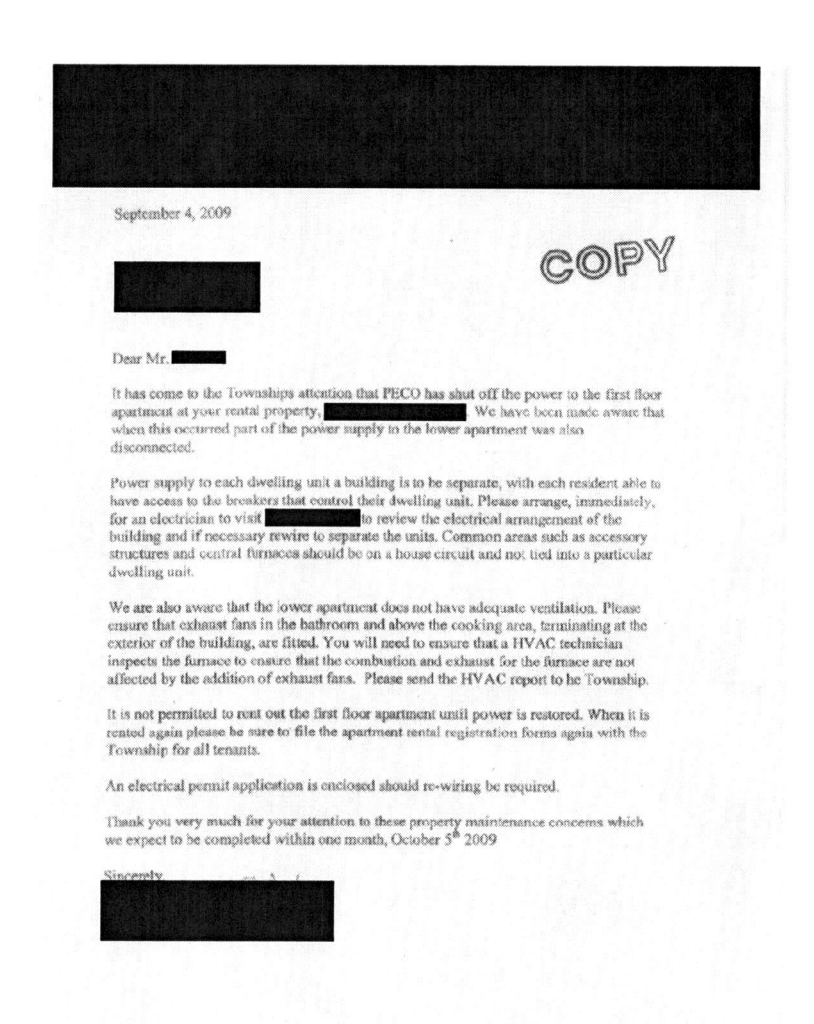

September 4, 2009

COPY

Dear Mr. ▮

It has come to the Townships attention that PECO has shut off the power to the first floor apartment at your rental property, ▮. We have been made aware that when this occurred part of the power supply to the lower apartment was also disconnected.

Power supply to each dwelling unit a building is to be separate, with each resident able to have access to the breakers that control their dwelling unit. Please arrange, immediately, for an electrician to visit ▮ to review the electrical arrangement of the building and if necessary rewire to separate the units. Common areas such as accessory structures and central furnaces should be on a house circuit and not tied into a particular dwelling unit.

We are also aware that the lower apartment does not have adequate ventilation. Please ensure that exhaust fans in the bathroom and above the cooking area, terminating at the exterior of the building, are fitted. You will need to ensure that a HVAC technician inspects the furnace to ensure that the combustion and exhaust for the furnace are not affected by the addition of exhaust fans. Please send the HVAC report to the Township.

It is not permitted to rent out the first floor apartment until power is restored. When it is rented again please be sure to file the apartment rental registration forms again with the Township for all tenants.

An electrical permit application is enclosed should re-wiring be required.

Thank you very much for your attention to these property maintenance concerns which we expect to be completed within one month, October 5th 2009

Sincerely

IN THE COURT OF COMMON PLEAS OF ▌▌▌▌ COUNTY, PA
CIVIL ACTION – LAW

▌▌▌▌▌▌▌▌▌▌▌▌ : NO. 09-30338
:
vs :
:
PAULIE SWIST :

ORDER

AND NOW, this 19th day of March, 2010, upon consideration of the Plaintiff's Petition for the Release of Escrow Funds, the rental payments made by the Defendant pursuant to his Notice of Appeal from the Order for Payment of Rent and Ejectment, same payments being made to the Prothonotary pursuant to Rule 1008(Pa. R.C.P.M.D.J.), shall be remitted immediately to the Plaintiff by the Prothonotary after so deposited, and shall be remitted on a monthly basis, if and when received from the Defendant during the pendency of this action.

It is further ORDERED and DECREED that the Plaintiff shall have right of access to the leased premises, after giving a seventy-two (72) hour notice in written form by mail and hand-delivered to the Defendant.

BY THE COURT:

A copy of this Order was mailed
on 03/22/10 via First Class Mail to:

Judicial Secretary

⇒ PECO.

PECO an Exelon Company
Customer Service Center

December 9, 2009

Paul A Swist

Dear Mr Swist;

In order to arrange an investigation for possible foreign wiring PECO will you will need to provide access to you're your unit, Bsmt apt and and also for the 1st fl apt. Once you can provide access we will be aBle to schedule an appointment for a PECO representative to come out to verify if there is foreign wiring

¡ATENCIÓN!

ÉSTE ES UN MENSAJE MUY IMPORTANTE. SI USTED NO LO ENTIENDE, FAVOR DE LLAMAR AL NÚMERO DE TELÉFONO QUE APARECE EN ESTE DOCUMENTO.

Sincerely,

Revenue Management

ELECTRICAL CONTRACTOR
SPECIALIZING IN ELECTRONIC BURGLAR & FIRE ALARMS

Paul Swist   Aug 2 2010

Under inspection The wires For The HotWater heater And Furnance And Line To The Garage ARe connected To The Basement Fuse panel. ALSo The Bathroom and m-d room ARe on The First Floor meter

8/17/10

Mr. Paul Swist

THIS IS NOTICE TO ALLOW AT+T PHONE Co. TO ENTER PROPERTY ON FRI. 8/20/10 BETWEEN 8 AM. AND 5 P.M. OR LANDLORD WILL ALLOW ACCESS WITH SUPERVISION. WORK TO BE DONE FOR 2ND FLOOR TENANT.

9/17/10

Mr. Swist

THIS IS THE 2ND NOTICE, TO ALLOW AT&T PHONE CO TO ENTER PROPERTY ON 9/15 BETWEEN 8 AM AND 12 P.M. WITH LANDLORD SUPERVISION. AND INSP. OF ENTIRE APT. FOR NEW TENANTS ALSO SAME DAY VARIOUS TIMES. PLEASE CALL ███████████ TO CONFIRM.

IF NO PHONE CONFIRMATION REC'D LANDLORD WILL BE ARRIVE WITH POLICE ESCORT AGAIN. @ 8 A.M. ON 9/15/10

February 10, 2010

CERTIFIED MAIL 7006 0810 0005 6691 5147

Dear Mr.

This is a follow up letter to the one sent to you dated September 4, 2009. Your tenant, Mr. Paul Swist has been to our office to inform us that there has been no action taken by you to correct the property maintenance concerns on your property. The concerns are as follows: (1) The power supply to each unit has not been separated; (2) The kitchen and bathroom ventilation has not been installed. The HVAC system needs to be inspected and a report submitted to verify that the additional exhaust does not affect the combustion and exhaust ventilation for the furnace. A permit will be required for any ventilation and electrical work done.
A written response is required from you within 5 days of receipt of this notice as to your intentions concerning this matter.

Yours in safety,

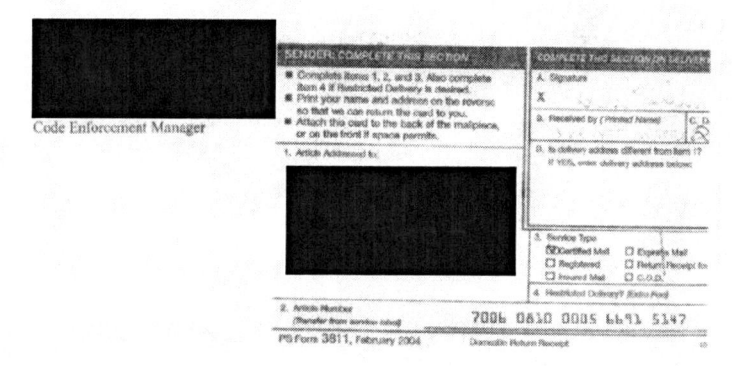

Code Enforcement Manager

34

As the weeks turned into months, and the court dates narrowed down, I pulled into the driveway and I saw a dude sitting on the tailgate of a pickup truck and another dude perched on the roof.
"You guys here for the bats?" I asked.
"There's bats here?" one of the men replied.
"Yes." I thought to myself-- *What could they be doing?,* and I mumbled something like "That dumb fuck Fay probably thinks I ran my R-6 cable up through the chimney." I just walked into the Hut, knowing that Mr. Wilson didn't give two flying fucks about that place, or its roof.
    I still chit-chatted with the old people next door from time to time. I told them that I would be moving in the near future. I asked them about Verizon being at their house. I knew why; I just wanted to hear what was up. The lady began to explain it to me, and she started to laugh. They had been out there for three days till 8 PM and talking with their technicians in Ohio.

"Paulie," she asked, "you know what they said the problem is?"

I just gave a smile and an eye roll.

"The alarm system."

We laugh together. The bottom line was that these Verizon guys aren't trained in looking for a magnetic field of triangulation. I felt bad for her and her husband. She knew I had to do what I was out to accomplish. We ended our conversation with a hug.

As I was walking away, she said "Be safe, Paulie."

I turned my body and said "I'll be fine."

35

There are different kinds of "punks" -- and then you have "royalty punks!" The first floor and the second floor landlines' wiring was in the basement.

"How convenient for me," I whisper. I had one of those Einstein ideas: I went to Home Depot and purchased a linesman phone. I waited for the right time, when Teddy wasn't home. I didn't know whether my plan was going to work.

If you don't try, you'll never know.

So I took it out of the package. There were two alligator clips attached to the phone. On one clip, the wire was red; on the other, black. The landline wiring in the basement was ancient. I was laughing to myself -- "crazy Paulie" -- as I nodded my head upward to where the wiring was and clipped my acquisitions to the brass screws. I flipped the switch on the linesman phone... nothing. I moved the clips over to another spot and flicked the switch again. This time, the phone produced a dial tone! Being persistent pays off, and anyone who knows me knows that I am just that.

"Shit, this is good!"

I simply waited for good old Teddy to come home. When he did, I gave him some time to get situated. I wondered whether I needed my equipment. Teddy's voice was loud for that of a little man and the ducts in the basement carried his voice well, if you know what I mean. As I had my phone ready to eavesdrop on the eavesdropper and to introduce Mr. Royalty Punk into my plan, I heard Teddy's voice through the ducts. He could have been on his cell or his landline so I flicked the switch over and I heard a second voice-- one that wasn't Teddy's.

"It's Fay," I realized.

They chit-chatted until Fay went into details and strategic plans. I was listening to this and thinking that it was good... really good. I heard Fay mention my name. He wasn't a happy camper.

"Oh well," I said to myself.

I took the clips off the brass screws and put the phone away until later. As I was making something to eat, I had to laugh. It was hysterical. Fay couldn't imagine in a hundred years that I would eavesdrop on him. That was all fine and dandy but what was more important was how he maneuvered the following day. When Teddy got home, I was waiting. I got my chair, pencil, pad, and protein bar. I heard Teddy's voice through the ducts and flipped the switch. You know whose voice I heard again. As I was taking notes, I was saying, "You dirty motherfuckers." Then I heard Fay say something really corny. I almost choked on my protein bar laughing. I had to be careful; if I made the wrong noise, he could have heard me. This went on for a couple of weeks. I archived and transcribed what I needed. Finally, it was time for "Royalty to become Reality!" It was like sticking an enema up his ass.

36

    I decided I needed some time out. It was the time of the 2009 Philadelphia Flyers playoffs. I went to this new upscale restaurant in King of Prussia. It wasn't a sports bar, but I knew the game would be on. There was a spot at the bar and a view of both the game and two attractive females right next to me... how convenient.
    They both gave me a polite look and I gave one back. As I was watching the game, one of the girls kept mentioning <u>The Color Purple</u>. The t-shirt that I was wearing throughout the game just happened to be that color. I just gave her a casual look and a smile. She was a good-looking chick. Towards the third period, I started a conversation.
    Talking to both of them, I asked their names, and they asked me mine. During the game, I overheard that one of the girls had a boyfriend. Soon after the game, the duo decided to leave. I followed them.
    They drove separate cars, of course, so I elected to follow the single girl. Her car was parked right next to mine. I said it

was an "omen." She laughed, got into her car, started it up, lowered her window, and began talking to me. I wasn't pushy or anything like that.

After five minutes, I asked her for her number.

"You're not going to call," she replied. I had this notion in my head that only a fool wouldn't call. She was 25, had no kids, and she made the cover of a popular fitness magazine. She was persistent about whether or not I would call. Ultimately, she told me to call her anytime after 9 AM. I gave her a nice, sentimental look, and got into my car. She waited for me to pull away. She was right behind me when her turn came up. She flashed her lights at me.

On Saturday, I called her -- Diane -- at about 12 noon. I used the cell phone of some dude at the gym. He was one of my boys; I trusted him. But the call went right to voicemail.

"Interesting," I said. I understood Fay's tactics from both the past and the present, but I wasn't going to jump the gun just yet. What I did know was that, at the bar, both girls kept their cells right in front of them, just as every female does.

That evening, I went to a pay phone and called at around 7 PM. Same thing-- right to voicemail. I tried again at midnight.

I repeated this over a 10-month span... about seven times in all.

37

 Later in this story, I'll describe what Fay's capable of doing with his cellular technology. But first... that stunt he fuckin' pulled. This is where royalty comes into play.
 Back in the basement with the linesman phone, I waited for a day when Teddy wasn't home. I put the clips on the brass screwed and I dialed Diane's number. It went straight to voicemail, as usual. About two minutes later, the linesman phone rang. I didn't say anything. I just slowly unclipped it and returned to the Hut.
 Though Fay had the technology right in front of him, he couldn't trace from where that call had come. I went back into the basement with a screwdriver and dismantled Teddy's phone system. I heard that Fay was livid over that. He was probably having an aneurysm.
 Now *that* is what you call a "Royalty Punk."

38

When Mr. Wilson decided to get involved with Fay, health issues came with it. There were periods of time Mr. Wilson would stop by, for one reason or another, but there were also lapses of time during which I didn't see him at all. It was in the beginning of this bullshit when, one day, I noticed two air casts around his feet. I looked at them a little weirdly.

I had to ask, "What happened, Mr. Wilson?" He began telling me that he was on a ladder at his house and, the next thing he knew, he was sliding all the way down. He cracked both of his feet. "Damn, Mr. Wilson, that must have hurt." I chuckled to myself.

Another time, his arm was in a sling. I asked what happened.

"Car accident," he responded. I laughed again!

Still another time, his fingers were in a splint. I asked again for an explanation. He told me that someone hit his car from behind.

And there was one more time when I saw him getting out of his car as I was leaving my Hut. I looked at him and his demeanor wasn't right.

"No cast of any kind," I said to myself. I decided to engage him in conversation. "What's up, Mr. Wilson?"

"I can't talk, Paulie. I have laryngitis."

When you know me as a person, you'll understand how I roll. Sometimes I can hold back my laughter but, considering these incidents with Mr. Wilson, I just couldn't help myself.

39

For over a six-week period, Mr. Wilson left three notes on my door pertaining to the second-floor tenant phone line. One note read, "AT&T needs to check the phone lines with landlord supervision. Get back to me ASAP."

"Yeah, right," I said, and I started to laugh.

Another note read "This is a reply to your request. I have an appointment. Therefore, we will have to reschedule for a later date. As you know, each unit should have its own dwelling unit access. P.S.: You probably want to get an exterminator for bugs."

A few days later, Mr. Wilson stopped by. I opened the door and I saw that he was holding a gallon of bug spray with an attachment sprayer... something you would purchase at Lowe's or Home Depot. He asked me what kind of bugs there were. All I said was "Bugs." I really wanted to say "electronic ones." So as he was spraying, not looking downward, but upward, I simply looked at him.

You're retarded, I thought. Same thing with the Friendly Environment stickums that stuck to his sneakers.

Mr. Wilson was familiar with the phone wiring; it was, after all, his apartment. He just wanted to see whether it had been tampered with.

During this period, I avoided him. A judge had ordered that Mr. Wilson was required to give me 72 hours' notice. The landlord caught on to that. So, when he mentioned another possible date, I said I had a doctor's appointment. I also put a padlock on the door. It wasn't just your ordinary lock-- it was a 21st-century combination without the numbers and no key entry. It was impossible to bypass that lock unless someone was to cut it or break down the door. Just in case someone got slick, I epoxied the screws on the lock and on the hinge. I knew that, in the past, they had come into my apartment on several occasions.

My court dates were reduced and I came to understand Fay's technology, triangulation, and surveillance program. Let it be known that it's deadly. I can't emphasize that enough. If you don't know for what you're looking, your life will get a 360-degree spin... or go to jail.

40

"Program." It comes down to this line of sight that means what it sounds like with cell towers. Radio modem, modules, and antennas omni or yagi... a certain frequency is required, and it's dependent on the signal and how far it needs to go. 2.4 GHz is for short range and clarity; 900 MHz is for long range. Let's say Fay is going for the long range and there's no building or structures obstructing the signal. His wireless cameras will give him a clear picture. It's tricky-- all of them out there are the slaves, and they have to send their digital signal back to the master modem. That's where the yagi and omni antennas come into play. They are very important in the wireless age. With regard to the video and audio devices, the antennas could be internal or external. Let's say Fay set up only one device. He would use yagi-to-yagi in multiple devices. The omni is the master and the yagis are the slaves pointing at the omni. This is only the tip of the iceberg. His PC video is a different ballgame; this runs through the fiber optics. Analog and digital are both used. Fay's options with this span out. It's like "Star Trek" meets "The Outer Limits."

Here is an example (and common sense) about the receivers hanging from the streetlights. I am not a technician by any means. When you're driving down a street, you can't miss them, though they should be unnoticeable. If I was to design a receiver of that nature, I would have the mechanism fabricated inside the streetlight with an internal omni antenna. That way, there would be no view of the receiver. Common sense.

Fay didn't like when I moved my cell phone booster antenna to different locations on or around the property. He would have very much appreciated it had I left it in one spot. I hardly did that. Fay's only option was to turn it down or up. Let's say I attached the R-6 cable to my TV and laid it out 50 yards with no antenna. You will double the power; I shouldn't have had any reception whatsoever.

When Fay turns it up -- or, should I say, when his frequency surrounds the end of the cable -- that's when a clear picture appears on all of my channels.

Let's go deeper into the subject. Ringtones are involved in triangulating. When you take different frequencies to pinpoint the area, once Fay has one of his stooges at the site with his cell phone, he can now direct the frequency to that particular spot and simply wait for his target to come. Once he has that signal, it's demodulated into a cell number. Now, electronically, that phone is Fay's. The victim may physically own that phone, but, in reality, that person has no idea that it is no longer his.

How did I come to understand the ringtones? One way was through one of my receivers. The other was the tape recorder. At my new place, I could see the tower from my kitchen area. The windows acted as amplifiers, so when I put the tape recorder at the window, ringtones could be heard... but, on the flipside, when that rhythm isn't consistent and is instead out of sync-- well, then you'll have problems.

That's when Paulie comes into play and takes a receiver and a TV and runs it through the R-6 cable or phone line. Because I did that, Fay's signal basically hitched a ride through the copper wire, and the ringtones went out of sync. It was useless when I did that. I was listening to the tape recorder, waiting for his system to choke up. When that occurs, he has options -- send one of his stooges down with their cell phone, wait until my TV is normal and I don't have anything hooked up -- it's a hassle to him, but he still has the advantage.

There are many ways to triangulate someone's cell phone and retrieve their signal. But there are also ways to identify its characteristics. On the other hand, sure, you could use a receiver. You could also use a tape recorder. It's easy. Get a Jupiter Jack, which is actually used for your cell phone-- when you're driving, the signal is broadcast through your stereo. What you would do in this case would be to plug the Jupiter Jack into the tape recorder, put your radio on FM 99.3, turn it up, and place the recorder in your sun visor, the sun visor being the highest available point. You will also need a 3.5 mm mono plug; the Jupiter plug is too small for the tape recorder. Now, when you're driving, and you know the sound for which you're looking, you'll hear it. It's the same method as in finding a GPS tracking device.

Two weeks until I move. More drama to follow.

41

My last court date. But not with Mr. Wilson. It was an early one, set for 9 AM. I filed a civil matter against the code enforcement manager for $1,200. I knew he would be last. This code enforcement manager took over from the previous one who initiated the first report against Mr. Wilson. I was up at this manager's office four different times to address my living conditions. For one reason or another, he was not following up on it. That's when I said "Let it be in the courtroom." I didn't know how to come up with a dollar amount for my judgment.

When Mr. Wilson kept leaving notes on my door stating that AT&T needed to come in and service the phone line, that was my avenue into the courtroom.

The first code enforcement manager said in the letter "_No one can move in until each unit has its own dwelling unit._" That meant "phone lines." Now that I had my avenue, I needed a dollar amount for which to sue, because it was an inconvenience to my living conditions. It's considered "a not happy environment apartment." The bottom line is "Do you want someone knocking at your door and leaving notes?" I came up with two months' rent. In reality, I didn't care about the money; I just wanted to have my day in that courtroom and see him lie as I questioned him.

So we were in the district courtroom. He had a lawyer and old Paulie, as usual, just had himself. As I was still standing, taking my paperwork out and placing the pictures flat on the table and in order, the judge entered the room. Both the code enforcement manager and his lawyer stood up and greeted the judge, and I followed suit.

I was still standing -- and so was the judge -- when he said "Mr. Swist, you cannot sue the code enforcement manager. If you would like to appeal, you may."

And then I heard a "Thank you, Judge" from the attorney. I chuckled briefly before thanking the judge myself.

Damn, I thought to myself. *I just set a new world record for the fastest court hearing of all time.* It had lasted a mere 20 seconds... if that.

Fay holds his own record for the most punks, or for punking himself. Now, I have one, also. I would much rather be impressed with mine than with his any day.

In my opinion, the judge should have stated some kind of legal precedent that delineated precisely why I couldn't sue. Or the code enforcement manager's lawyer should have been the one making that case, if it did, in fact, exist.

As I was walking out the door, the code enforcement manager was standing there. I put my hand out and said "No hard feelings."

In the end, it was a win for me!

42

One last week at the Hut, and one more knock at my door. It was a weekday-- 9 AM sharp. Typically, no one ever came over on such a day at such an hour. I threw on a shirt and opened the door. When I looked up, I saw four health inspectors, two township police officers, and the landlord. (Sounds like that Christmas carol, "The Twelve Days of Christmas.")

Anyway, a month earlier, I had discovered mold in my bathroom. I smiled at the mold with a shitty smirk and said to myself, "Mr. Wilson, that's a hazard toward your tenant!" The pipes leaked behind the shower wall. As Paulie says, "That's another avenue to stick up his ass."

It was about a month prior that I had taken pictures of the mold and given part of this evidence to the Board of Health. I put everything in a manila envelope and hand-delivered it. It was all I could do at that point.

I welcomed them in-- two females and two dudes. They had a camera and took pictures while the officers waited outside. Mr. Wilson was uptight. The health inspectors were only there for 15 minutes; Mr. Wilson was subsequently ordered to remove the mold, and he had only so many days to do it.

Mr. Wilson had no reason to bring two township police officers along. I'd questioned him at a previous court date as to whether I'd ever threatened him, and his response was "No question." When I asked why he felt it was appropriate to bring them to a health inspection, he claimed that I intimidated him. I reminded him that all such matters were civil, not criminal.

As I shook the inspectors' hands and thanked them, I gave a loud whisper to the dude.

"It's like being at Area 51."

He didn't know what to say.

43

About five days later, at around the same time of day, I heard a knock at the door. That time, only two inspectors and the landlord were there to pay a visit.

These people don't play around, I thought to myself. As Mr. Wilson was scraping and tearing out part of the drywall, he looked at one of the inspectors to get his OK. He said that still more had to be taken out. I was laughing -- I couldn't hold it back -- but my mind had flashbacks of my son, and memories of Mr. Wilson lying about my boy in the courtroom.

A few more days, and I'd be out. Later that evening, I could tell by the way the TV was reacting that Fay was trying to tune his frequencies in on my cable. Though it was dark, I had a gut feeling, and I went outside, down the driveway, only to find two dudes standing there, one smoking a cigarette and the other using his cell phone. I approached them.

"What are you doing?" I asked, and the bigger of the two stuttered something out. "What is wrong with you?"

He replied that he had a stuttering problem.

"Not that," I said, stifling a laugh. "You guys can't be here. It's 9 PM." They had even parked in the driveway. The smaller dude said he was thinking about renting one of the apartments.

"At nine o'clock at night?" I asked. "And you're standing by my cable. Get out of here."

"Well," sneered the little dude, "I wouldn't want *you* as a neighbor." I just looked at them. How lame could Fay's surveillance become? How half-assed could his triangulation get?

I locked up the Hut and went back to the police station, where I said to an officer that "You may or may not know what's been going on at my residence, but I am here this evening to give you a heads-up. If another person comes onto my driveway and plays dumb, I am gonna hurt him." With that, I walked out the station's doors. Again.

44

I was up early. The movers were scheduled for 8 AM but the previous night had been a rough one. Dreams work in mysterious ways; some you can remember, and others you can't, unless something triggers a memory of it. Maybe my adrenaline was increasing my blood rapidity. Who knows?

Anyway, I don't know if it happened at the gym, but that seems more than likely. Right in the beginning of 2008, when all of this bullshit started, there was a particular evening during which I noticed on Zorro all these white spots around his eyes, ears, and his body (his back, to the exclusion of his underside). I didn't know what to make of it.

So, the next day, I made an appointment with the vet to have him checked out. We were greeted by the veterinarian. She liked Zorro. She also knew I was a very protective person. I guess she may have understood the character within me.

"I don't know," she said, examining him. "Maybe age. It's just the pattern of the spots and how they're snow white." She ended the checkup by saying "He'll be just fine, Paul." I said "Okay" and shook her hand.

The next day, I got a phone call. It was the veterinarian. She began to tell me that some sort of acid had been thrown at Zorro. At that moment, I looked down at my boy. The vet mentioned that she hadn't wanted me driving home upset and I respected her decision. I thanked her and hung up.

As my mind was backtracking, bitterness bubbled within me. "Okay, motherfucker," I said.

A month went by. I didn't say anything to anybody. I just went about my business and carried on with my routine. I guessed that, if I just played it out or remained cool about the situation, maybe the person responsible would strike again and his ass would be mine.

Little did I know that, some months down the road, I found out about Zorro being poisoned.

On many occasions, I've taken him to the dog park. People would ask me about the white spots on him. Some I would tell what happened, while to others I chalked it up to age.

So I said to my boy, "Daddy gonna fix you up." I went to CVS and purchased some Just for Men jet-black hair dye. I applied it to the spots and waited five minutes before rinsing off Zorro's fur. He shook off the remaining water. I started to towel-dry him-- he always enjoyed it when I gave him a bath. If there was water in one of his ears, he would tilt his head and let me know if I didn't do a good enough job of getting it out. The hair dye did the trick, but not completely. The spots were just too white.

With each passing day, my guard was raised. I couldn't oversee Zorro every hour, especially if someone knows my routine-- and somebody did.

It ate at me how someone could stoop so low.

This one day, I arrived at the gym. There were some construction workers on the outskirts of the gym. I'd seen them from time to time. That day, though, I was out to take someone's head off. I approached the dudes and began to ask them if they ever saw anybody throw anything at Zorro. I informed them that whoever had done it must have had the acid in a cup and a five-foot distance between them, because of the pattern of injury. I then reached into my sweats and pulled out $10,000. I threw it on the ground right in front of them and said "Look. This could be yours, no questions asked. Tell me if you know anybody or have seen anything. Let me know, and it's yours."

They just looked at each other. I picked up my money and walked away. I never did find out anything.

About three weeks later, after the incident with Zorro, Fay was diagnosed with a tumor behind his left eye.

The movers arrived. I didn't have a lot of possessions-- enough to get on in life. My furniture reflected my character: brass, oak, copper. Most of it I altered to my satisfaction.

Everything was loaded up within an hour's time. Everyone knows moving is a bitch. It sucks.

My guard was not down... not by any means. When a person spends millions in finances and manpower, and the truth comes out, it doesn't take a rocket scientist to put it all together.

45

My new place was in King of Prussia, about 15 minutes from the Hut. It's an upscale town, with one of the biggest shopping malls in the States. I lived in a house converted into two apartments; mine was on the second floor and was a whole lot bigger than the Hut had been. Cheaper, too. One of my friends had hooked me up with it.

I had the place lined up for a couple of months. I didn't let anybody know where I was moving. One person did know-- but what he didn't know was that I was setting him up to get "punked" again.

Fay thought I would simply whip out my cell and make my calls at my new apartment.

That's his problem. He thinks -- he assumes -- that things are going to go his way. You can't run a so-called "investigation" like that. It's like hoping to hit the Powerball. In his mind, he was hoping that, one day, I'd cross that line, one way or another.

I slowly unpacked and got situated. It's not my style to do everything at once. I guess it's like foreplay. On top of that, I had to find a new gym.

For the time being, I stuck it out at my old gym, until I found one that would suit my needs. It was a pain in the ass to get there, considering the traffic. There were only two routes. So my routine somewhat started everybody's routine one way or another, but I noticed something for a few days in a row: a car sitting on an overhead bridge. I knew what was up.

If I was on my cell and drove under the bridge, my signal or RF would only go one way... up. The dude in the car would be talking on his cell phone and Fay keeps that area triangulated. The only signal he got after I went under the bridge was the thought that he had gotten punked again.

46

    To triangulate, it takes a number of components, a system that is prepared to handle that type of software, cell towers, and an array of frequency ranges.
    I only know how to detect and identify characteristics in that I know how they can be used. Cell phone boosters are in the past. Don't get me wrong-- it's a good choice, but more conventionally, I used my Camera Hunter. It's deadly. I used it way beyond the purpose for which it was meant. Believe it or not, it was perfect. Small, compact, durable, accurate, and having a sensitive frequency range of 900 MHz to 2.4 GHz.
    The stock antennae, on a scale from one to 10, was a six. I was a bit familiar with upgrading my Camera Hunter. I obtained a magazine for antenna upgrades.
    I also knew that someone was waiting for me to place my order.
    Earlier that day, I had purchased an American Express gift card worth $50. I knew I was just setting it up. Later, around 3 PM, I went to the gym. I saw this dude that worked there and I

asked him if I could use his cell to order a 900 MHz antenna out of the magazine that I showed him. He said it was okay, so I placed my order. The antenna was worth $30, not including shipping. I asked how long it would be until I received my antenna and was told that it would arrive within a week's time. I thanked the representative, and I thanked the dude for letting me use his cell.

The next day, the dude's cell phone was hacked and all his Facebook information was gone. He never found out who took it. But I know who!

Fay had assumed again. He knew I had an interest in this magazine; it was from a counter-surveillance company. What he thought was that I would use one of my own cell phones to place the order. Ahead of time, he used the authority of his badge to place a call to this company and basically give them a heads up: If Paul Swist places an order, from what number is he calling? The company would then relay the information back to Fay.

He thought the dude's cell phone had been my own. I had used it one time, and one time only. Fay took the dude's information and checked it to see whether any names or other information popped into his mind.

Only to find out that -- yep, that's right -- he got punked again.

It was a $50 punk and, on top of that, I never received my antenna, or heard anything about it.

I didn't need to order the antenna after all. I made my own. It wasn't easy; it took me a couple of months of toying and putting my attempts through different tests to make sure I was getting the right output.

My Camera Hunter (receiver) was good. Too much antenna would drown it out. The fittings had to be properly filed to achieve what I needed for a suitable antenna. I needed one for 900 MHz and another for 2.4 GHz. After all was said and done with the antennae, mine would outperform any of its after-market brethren. The time I put into them had paid off big time!

I already had places in mind, I knew how Fay maneuvered, and -- most of all -- I understood the frequency band for which to look. As I said before, there are different networks. That means 3 Gs. Faster data. Of course Fay would choose that. He needed his information quickly, so I would do a before-and-after check. I knew the band on which to concentrate. Say I went to a Wal-Mart. I'd do a check, and nothing. Twenty minutes later, I would come out, turn on the Hunter, and tune it into the band RF, and bingo! Not only that, but my eyes would roam around, and two cars over I would see a dude or woman on their cell, doing the obvious.

I want you, the reader, to understand that I can't go into details. For me to map it out and go into great detail-- I can't, for reasons of good law enforcement and respect for the technology and its purpose.

I look back, when my brother and I had the compass up to the ceiling, and not understanding... just looking at each other. What actually was occurring was that the Hut was drowned in electricity. Part of the ceiling had a very fine chicken wire in the plaster. It was attached to the drywall. You could stick anything metal near a probe and it would beep the same thing repeatedly. Same thing at my new place. I have these old radiators, the cast-iron ones. Sometimes I can be a foot away and it sets it off. Same thing with my bathtub. It's an old-fashioned one and not fiberglass... same beep. All Fay knows as to what to do is to turn it up and down.

It's like that commercial for Planet Hollywood Fitness.

It's the same principle as if someone were to log onto your cell and the signal bars would go down, then plateau out. The battery would drain faster because more energy is being used.

Just like my car battery.

47

    Here is a profile of Fay's past and present. When all is said and done, it comes down to his ego. As you read this story, remember that he doesn't care how many people he dragged into his "witch hunt." His attitude paints a perfect picture of how far and how low his mentality will go to suit his needs.

    After I left Gold's Gym, it closed down due to mismanagement. I had to find another gym that was convenient. There was one in this shopping center; I checked it out and joined. I ran into some dudes I knew. Just so you know, a gym is like a beauty salon-- gossip, people talking, stuff like that. Anyway, I ran into this one dude, Drew. I'd known him for over 15 years or so, and we have our share of nostalgic stories, including when Fay used to juice steroids up and start talking.

    If you were to ask Fay in this day and age whether he'd ever juiced, he would deny it. Back in the day, though, it was a known big deal. Everybody was darting up syringes on the floor. Dudes' sweats would have blood markings on them. There were about 75 users and Fay was one of them.

Next thing I knew, Drew was telling me how a relative had called him up to request a conversation in person. His cousin had made it clear that it was in his best interest to stay away from a certain female.

"You know my cousin," said Drew. "He'll set your ass up."

"It would be best to lose the number," I replied.

Now, from time to time, Drew dipple-dappled in the fast lane. So he took the advice and moved on to another chick.

I didn't understand what had actually occurred until I started to explain about Fay's eavesdropping with cellular technology and video surveillance. Drew started to backtrack in his mind and he said "Motherfucker, that brick!"

"See?" I said. "And I'll make it more black-and-white for you." She was probably talking to one of her girlfriends about how she had met this guy, a good-looking bodybuilder with a child. Meanwhile, Fay's listening in, and he sees you as a threat. Obviously, he can't confront you. Of course she's not going to mention anything to Fay. So he gets his cousin to do the dirty work for him. It wasn't as if Fay could say he was eavesdropping.

The other point is that he had the capabilities to hack into any store that had video surveillance, as long as their system was tied into the police station.

I hate to say it, but he had been stalking her. That's sad-- real sad.

Which brings me to those times I was at grocery stores or other shopping destinations. This didn't happen just a few times... it happened many, many times over.

What was Fay's objective? That's on him! I would see his stooges repeatedly and I knew about his Peeping Tom nature. So I figured that, if he acted like a bitch, I would treat him as one. As I was pushing my cart, I went into the female aisle and loaded it up with maxi pads, douche, tampons... "the works." Then I parked the cart right under the dome camera and grabbed my other stuff, leaving the cart behind.

The way he operates an investigation is beyond me. This bullshit went on for a couple of years.

Before Drew and I went our separate ways, I said to him, "I think, back in the day, Fay was injected with estrogen. He sure acts like a bitch."

Fay never, in his life, could imagine this could come out. Why would it? There's an old saying: "Water under the bridge."

But there's another part. A dam was built and all that water backed up and took out the bridge. I built that dam!

On top of that, you can see that he doesn't respect other law enforcement. The probation officer? He used him, and local police, to alter a police report. What if Mr. Wilson had a heart attack from the stress of it all? Don't get me wrong-- Mr. Wilson is the type of person who, if he can get one over on you, he'll take that advantage. He's a bullshitter. I've seen that in the past, with previous tenants. I, on the other hand... I put him on the spot, and the other tenants saw it.

Some people came up to me and said "Damn, Paulie! You broke Fay down!" I said that he had it coming to him. But then I thought, *How can I make it up to him?* I could ask him for a group photo, with him wearing his tarnished badge. Or a gift of some kind. I could give him the tape recorder, but he might have flashbacks. Then it came to me-- the perfect gift. A bobblehead doll. He could put it on his fireplace mantel or his dashboard and watch it bop around.

48

At my new place, I came to meet the tenants below me. They were a dude and his girlfriend. A few days after I moved in, I passed on to him part of this story. His reaction was, basically, "That's wild." As the months passed by, we had brief conversations. One time, we were talking, and I changed the subject to ask him about his cell phone. Was he getting a lot of text messages and unusual calls? He said that he was-- sometimes six in a row, coming from odd numbers he didn't recognize. I then explained to him what was occurring. Every time I jammed Fay's signal, it took the ringtone out of rhythm, and it would have to be recalibrated. There were a few ways Fay could get things back on track, and the solution could be as simple as your cell phone.

After I explained what the ringtone was, and how pinging his cell worked, I went into more detail about Fay's surveillance. I pointed to the telephone pole in front of our apartments. I told the dude that Fay had to know when I was leaving and that, since there was only one exit, his lone option was a motion sensor. But there was also a trip sensor. In other words, if I was walking down my steps, at the bottom of the stairs, I would activate the trip sensor. It would send a text message or SMS e-mail to notify Fay that motion had been identified. Then he would track me through video.

There was IP video, wireless... he could even use the PennDOT systems, the ones on motor highways.

I even said that it went deeper than that, but I didn't want to hold him up, and we split off into our own respective apartments.

To demonstrate this technology, I would ask that you imagine this scenario. Let's say Moammar Gadhafi was aware of the cellular triangulation that had been imposed upon him. He wouldn't want anything to do with a cell phone for the obvious reasons involving the pinpointing of his whereabouts.

Let's say he had a niece or a daughter who had a cell phone. The military monitors her cell and listens in to find out she's going over to Uncle Gadhafi's house, not knowing her cell is being monitored. A voice analysis is done to hear if Mr. Gadhafi is present at the family gathering. Once it's confirmed, the military can program a cruise missile to take out its target, and he'll never see it coming.

But, on the other hand, Mr. Gadhafi could invest in a cell phone booster, and with a trained eye and a little patience, he could tell whether he was being triangulated.

From what I saw on the news, towers were being taken out -- not by our military, but by the terrorists. They knew about the technology. Not all of it, but, for the most part, it could have cost them their lead.

Common sense dictates that the military wouldn't strike the towers because of their obvious surveillance advantage.

49

Imagine yourself living your life the way I did. How would you handle it? When you read, you'll understand why this certain individual didn't want this book to be published.

I received a summons for one of my court hearings. I had been waiting for that date to come so that I could stick it up Mr. Wilson's ass. The morning before the hearing, it was really windy. You could hear the wind howling through the chimney. The next thing I knew, there were bees, maybe 20 or so. As I was opening the door to get them out, one caught me in the eye. I guess they were pissed. Well, my eye swelled completely shut. The only thing that went through my mind was that I wouldn't be able to see during court the following day.

I had to come up with a solution, and it wouldn't be postponing my court date.

I put some more though into the ordeal. I got dressed and ate my Cheerios. I thought to myself that, when people lose their sight all of a sudden, they finally realize how fortunate they had been to have two eyes to see.

It was time to put my driving skills to the test. It was awkward, but I succeeded. So my first stop was a health and nutrition store. I've been there many times, and I knew for what I was looking. When I entered the store, I knew both of the females that were working there.

"Oh my God," they both said, "what happened?"

"Bee sting," I replied. I then said that I needed a patch, and they hooked me up. I put it on right there and looked in the mirror. I started to laugh, and one of the employees said that it fit my image well. I didn't know how to take that, but I was satisfied.

My next stop was the gym. I wanted to get used to being around people. I guess it was my conscience. So, when I entered the gym, some dudes that I knew were working out and they looked at me kind of funny. I immediately lifted my eye patch and mentioned the bee sting. I didn't want anyone to think that I had gotten into a fight and got my ass whooped. You can tell when someone gets punched in the eye by the black circle. Anyway, I started into my workout and tanning as usual. I just wanted to be comfortable at the court hearing.

The next morning, I got up and my eye was still sealed shut. "It is what it is." I put the patch on and proceeded to the rest of my routine.

The hearing was scheduled for early: 9 AM. I arrived at the courthouse and entered the courtroom. Mr. Wilson and his lawyer were already present. They both gave me a double-take, but I didn't say anything. So, when the judge entered the room, the three of us stood up and greeted him. Mr. Wilson and his lawyer then sat back down. I, on the other hand, remained standing and explained the patch over my eye to the judge, lifting it so he could see my injury. He just made a face, a reaction that came off as "Damn, that must have hurt." The lawyer looked over to me at that second. I explained to the judge what happened.

I could see Mr. Wilson thinking to himself: *First the fucking bat, and now the bees. What next?* I simply shot him a quick grin.

During the hearing, I could see that the judge was a bit puzzled. Why would a landlord want to get rid of a tenant?

The judge was fair to me. It didn't go the way Mr. Wilson thought it would. The judge only ordered me to take the padlock off my door.

Later that evening, I mailed the judge a portion of this story, along with some documents. I wanted him to know that there was a whole lot more to the story than landlord and tenant issues, and that I just wanted a fair hearing.

The next week, I received a certified letter from Mr. Wilson stating that my rent would be raised to $1,200 a month.

After my last hearing with Mr. Wilson, I agreed to meet him at the Hut for an inspection and to return the key.

As I was waiting for him, I gathered some miscellaneous stuff and put it in my trunk. I heard a rumbling noise coming up the driveway. I couldn't see who was driving, as the windows were tinted. Mr. Wilson got out of the car; he was driving a brand new Chevy Camaro.

"Damn," I said. "You got a new car."

"It's a rental, Paulie."

"Mr. Wilson, you're bullshitting me."

"Alright, Paulie. I bought it."

"Damn," I repeated. He was proud of it.

We went inside the place. It needed to be cleaned up. Anytime someone moves, there's junk laying around. Mr. Wilson was bitching about the junk. He told me that I clearly didn't want my escrow.

"You keep it," I said, shooting him a cocky look.

So he checked everything out. I guess he thought that I would sabotage something. When he went into the bathroom, he opened the one trap door where the mold and corrosion had built up. He started messing around with one of the pipes. As I was watching him, it started to leak really badly. I was laughing, as usual. It was always something when he came over. He was trying to stop the leak. He asked me whether I had any tools.

"Yes and no," I said. "But I'm hungry. If you feed me, I'll give you a pair of pliers."

"I am not feeding you, Paulie."

I said "Then no pliers!" and started to laugh again. "Good-bye, Mr. Wilson. You and your new James Bond car."

50

 As I moved into my new place, there was a parade of drama and, of course, a new township chief officer to follow. I've known him for 15 years or so and, needless to say, he's a good man and an honest officer. He knows all about me and drug trafficking. From time to time, we work out at the same gyms and simply engage in small talk, shake hands, and go about our routines.
 As Fay led his stooges, it was like a circus parade, just one thing after another.
 I had no choice but to head up to the police station and talk to the Chief. I didn't want to put him in a situation, but on the other hand, I had to.
 When I entered, there was a female behind the glass.
 "Thank God," I mumbled to myself, "there's no little fat guy behind the glass." And I didn't feel like playing Wheel of Fortune again, so I asked for the Chief, but I had to make an appointment, so I did.

Two days later, I met with the Chief. When he came into the waiting room, I stood up to greet him and I shook his hand. We were always on a first-name basis. I followed him into a room and explained to him what had been going on.

I basically got right to the issues. I slid him a portion of this story.

"That's a lot to read," he said.

"I just wanted you to know what's been going on," I replied, "and the reasons why we're having this sit-down." I started to elaborate in detail about the video cameras on the telephone poles, especially the one in front of my apartment... how it worked with a motion sensor and then with WiFi encryption. I also mentioned to him about the time I ordered the 900 MHz antenna and what happened to the dude's information. I said that, on top of that, if he was to drive his vehicle within 20 yards of my home and put his stereo on AM 910, he would hear these tones for 10 seconds. Then they would stop, and then they'd repeat.

"Chief, for me to sit in front of you and make this claim... that's how sure I am. And it doesn't stop there." I told him about the Verizon dudes being out in front of my place repeatedly at some particular spots.

What I didn't tell the Chief was that I took a letter and part of this story down to Philadelphia, where Verizon's main building is, and delivered it to one of their lawyers. I didn't even go into detail when it switched hands; I just said that they might have wanted to be aware of what had been going on.

After I passed on that information, I never saw the loiterers again.

As I saw the Chief's body language absorbing what I was saying, I somewhat regretted putting him in such an awkward situation, but I offered for him to come to my residence.

"Paulie," he said, "if I stop over and you reveal everything, and then I go and talk to Fay and he says to me that he's running an investigation, I can't come back to you and confirm it."

"But you're the Chief of this township," I said, and he agreed.

I wasn't going to press up on him and make him feel uncomfortable, so I eased up a bit and asked him whether this was how an investigation should be handled. He answered in the negative and looked downward, disgusted.

When we stood up to shake hands, I felt a different impression from him... one that said "Paulie really stuck it up Fay's ass!"

51

As I walked out those doors, I noted that I hadn't mentioned other incidents that have occurred, like the time I saw these two survey dudes pull up across the street. As I was looking out the window, I saw that there was a company name on the truck; then I saw one dude on his cell and the other setting up a tripod with a scope attached. My eyes were focused on the one talking on his cell. I could tell by his body language and movements that he was approaching my property. At that time, I threw open the window.

"What the fuck are you doing?" I asked.

"Doing a survey," came the response. I closed the window, put my sneakers on, and went out to where their truck was. I wanted to hurt somebody, badly-- and not their feelings, if you know what I mean. I asked him again what he was doing and he repeats that he was surveying. The other guy was looking at me. I looked right back with a gaze that said "Dude, I would put a hurt on you." I glanced over to his companion and repeated "Do not come onto this property" three times. The dude asked why and I said that there had been a lot of robberies.

"We're going to be here all afternoon," he said.

"Don't," was all I said, and I drove my point home with a hard stare before going back inside.

Ten minutes later, the two dudes and their tripod were gone.

Same bullshit, just like Mr. Wilson and the rest of Fay's rejects.

Then, there was my local carrier. He reminded me of the guy in the movie _Deliverance_ -- the short, fat guy who got raped by the hillbillies. For about a four-month period, I noticed where he was stopping his mail truck on my street. It was a two-lane street. I also knew where the points were for the triangulation; by no means was I gawking out my windows. I could just tell by my how TV and other electrical appliances reacted. In other words, I became accustomed to it. Anyway, this one day in August, it was 90 degrees and humid at 3:30 or so in the afternoon. The local carrier stopped his truck with two wheels on my lawn. He got out and started to sweep his truck out with a whisk brush.

"What a nimrod," I said. After two minutes, he got back in his truck and moved it up a couple of feet, then repeated the sweeping bullshit again. He was in a full sweat. There was no shade and I could see his lips moving; he had a Bluetooth connected to his cell. This went on for about ten minutes.

Anyone that knows me knows that I'm a sweater. I hate the heat. That's probably why I didn't go out on that particular day.

Sneakers on again, and out the door I went. I went right up to him and asked him "Are you retarded?" When he replied with "No," I asked him why he pulled his truck onto my lawn... then start to sweep, stop, reenter his truck, move it, and start to sweep again. He didn't know what to say-- he merely gave me that dumb-and-dumber look.

Fay was probably laughing his ass off because the one video camera on the telephone pole overlooks the street and my apartment.

I went back inside. I was hoping that the local carrier would say something smart, but he didn't. I wasn't through with him yet.

A few days later, I headed over to Staples. That's where I always made my copies, as it was the cheapest. I passed a portion of this story to the clerk and asked for a single copy.

Back home I went. I wrote a letterhead to the Carrier Supervisor:

This is to inform you about one of your postal carriers and his actions. For a three-month period, the carrier has stopped around my property, and on this one particular spot, he parked one side of his truck on my lawn and started to sweep out his vehicle. After two minutes, he stops, moves a couple of feet, and starts sweeping again, while he's on his cell phone. The sole purpose of this action? He's being used by a detective from the county, one who's in charge of surveillance and cellular triangulation. You should also be aware that my street is a two-way. By him performing this act, there's a possible car accident waiting to happen. Now, this is my claim: If he wishes to be upfront with you, perhaps he could establish cell phone records for that timeframe. If you or any other supervisors would like me to show you or walk you through the surveillance technology, feel free to stop by.
Paul Swist

I put the letterhead and copied portion of my story in a manila envelope and hand-delivered it to the supervisor.

About a month later, that local carrier was gone.

52

    Fay truly thinks that I don't understand his surveillance program.
    Anything wireless, fiber optic, even copper cable, can be hacked or disrupted, whatever circumstances should come about.
    When the word "sound" comes to mind, it plays a major role.
    For example, if you were to throw a small pebble into a pond on a calm day, you'd see the ripple effect it gives off, because it's a sound wave.
    Now imagine this: Let's say that, when NASA fires a five thousand pound bomb at the moon to see whether any particulates consist of ice for future fuel, when the impact occurs, it gives off a sound wave. In my eyes, that's not good, because of meteorites and asteroids orbiting around other planets and moons. Once a shockwave ripple effect hits one, it knocks it off course. It's just like lightning-- when it hits something, first there's the shock, and then it's looking to ground out somewhere. By no means am I an

astronomer, but I do have common sense. The same thing for an earthquake. It strikes and can be felt for a very great distance.

What this boils down to is that any type of cable, including fiber optic (even though it works with light in a glasslike tube), is subject to these effects.

So I came up with a solution. I knew the box on the telephone pole was meant for me. First of all, I had never seen one look like that, especially that particular specimen. Its height was about 18 inches; it was eight inches wide and eight inches deep, with two cables exiting out of the bottom and feeding into another object on the cable lines. If one is driving, or simply looks out the front of his residence, he'd see that his local provider has a box on the pole for cable TV or internet, but it's about two inches thick and about 12 inches in length.

When I use my video camera, which has zooms of 40X and 800X, I put it to its greatest zoom setting. Let me tell you, when it zooms in on a spot from 30 yards away, it reveals everything to me.

"You slick motherfucker," I said to myself, "you're busted." That's where I had seen these manufacturer's logos in the lower-left corner, stamped out. They were only a quarter of an inch wide. I couldn't see the lens, but it made sense. It was even with my door and, needless to say, with my bathroom. If I were sitting on my toilet and there wasn't any curtain, Fay could see me sitting there, doing my business, just like at the Hut. The only difference was that he couldn't see me there. Pervert.

As I moved the toggle switch for the zoom function, I examined the rest of the box and noticed more words, these reading "Phone Company," but they were not punched out. With the naked eye, this would not have been evident.

I didn't stop there.

I knew that there was more going on behind the scenes than just the camera and its motion sensor. Both wires exiting out of the bottom were about a half-inch in diameter. Behind one wire was a rubber antenna; it was almost flush. I'd seen that setup before. Not with Fay, but with my own past research.

Now I understood Fay's technology and what was required for him to retrieve data.

At the Hut, when Mr. Wilson was so persistent in coming in and checking out Teddy's phone line... that's when I figured out what was needed to assist Fay's system. With that said, Teddy or one of Fay's stooges would basically use their cells to tune the signal in manually. Without the convenience of the phone line, that meant frustration for Fay.

At first, my thought was to just cut the two wires hanging from the bottom of the box.

So I went to Home Depot and arrived at the gardening department. I was looking for one of those poles that extended outwards 15 feet, with a sickle blade on the end. As I was walking down the aisle, I saw it. I smiled as I grasped it in my hand. I tore the plastic from the blade and pulled the rope to see what kind of damage it could inflict. I was satisfied.

I purchased it and headed home.

As I was getting out of the car, I knew Fay was watching me like the bitch he is. So I stood there like the Grim Reaper. I pulled the rope a couple of times and smirked before going inside.

Now, again, he assumed that I was going to stand right under the box and extend the sickle blade to cut the wires. I decline to do that, for I know of his other video camera on the opposing telephone pole, and its view of the one in question.

That's the way he likes to work his surveillance. He can maneuver the video.

I've experienced his games since the beginning of this bullshit. As an example, if I was out in front of my place with my receiver, and I was getting a reading that there was a video camera present, and if I was to walk towards it, then, all of a sudden, the reading would stop because Fay could see me through another camera. The bottom line was that he did not want his videos to be revealed.

But I had something in mind. Maybe Mother Nature would help me out. That's when the Grim Reaper would make his presence known.

Unfortunately, after three weeks... no fog.

So I returned the pole and got my money back.

"THE BOX"

53

Dreams work in mysterious ways, from far beyond to the present. Sometimes they even become reality.

To mystify this one evening, before I went to sleep, I had this idea of shooting the box out front of my apartment. As I was comatose, in a deep sleep, all these characters came out to play. It was like *Field of Dreams*.

Little green Mars dudes. Lee Harvey Oswald.

They were all giving their strategic input... who's doing this, what's that for, where am I. It was chaotic.

During this fantasy, I saw sparks, wind blowing, and a tremendous rainfall. Shots from a pellet rifle and Mr. Oswald in a sniper position.

It was so bizarre.

At the end of the dream, I asked my characters whether they thought I should give Thrill Seeker the air rifle as a present.

They all huddled up. I could hear some mumbo jumbo, some chatter.

Next thing I know, one of the Mars dudes says, "No, not a good idea. He might shoot his eye out." And they all started to bust out laughing. And Mr. Oswald asked me whether I'd ever seen _A Christmas Story_, where the kid had always wanted a BB gun, which he promptly shot into his eye.

As I joined in on the laughter, I noticed the Grim Reaper. He had the same smirk as I did. I tried to ask him "How?"

No words came out, but I read his lips. "I am watching over you."

I awoke the next morning. "Crazy dream," I said, and I went into the living room to look out the window. I turned to the mirror on the wall, and there was a reflection of that smirk.

54

The dream of my twilight hours returned as a daydream. I still had faith in Mother Nature. I knew she wouldn't let me down again... and she didn't. The dream had given me another idea. It just wasn't going to be as easy to execute. I went to a gun shop and purchased a pellet rifle. As a boy growing up, I had my share of BB and pellet guns. They were different back in the 70s. With today's technology, they have a whole lot more firepower. The price varies depending on the model and velocity. The one that caught my eye was one thousand with lead pellets and twelve hundred with PBA. What that means is that it's a different-alloy metal that flies about 40% more quickly. So the dude recommended certain pellets. They were top-of-the-line. I paid and walked out. When I returned to the parking lot, I turned on my Camera Hunter and tuned it into the frequency band that Fay used. He loved his WiFi video bullshit. He'd even travel towns away. I started to understand his ways, and it made sense: If there was a large shopping center, which this one was, it would be sensible to stick a video camera on a telephone pole overlooking the parking lot. That way, he could zoom in. In his manner of thinking, he would always be on top of that totem pole.

I hated to spoil his wishful thinking, but there was a new face on top, and we all know whose it is.

Now, when I got home, I wasn't going to be stupid and take the gun out or show the box it came in. Why? First of all, I didn't want my neighbors to see. I understand that it's only a pellet gun, but sometimes a minor issue of some kind can morph into something more extreme. Plus, I didn't want Fay to capture it on his video.

So I waited a couple of days and went to a remote area, opened up the trunk, and pulled the rifle out. I also secured a plastic kitchen trash can and a hacksaw blade, with which I started to cut the gun's barrel so that only ten inches would remain. I put the butt-end of the gun on the ground and pushed down on the barrel so that it folded, then I stuck it in the trash can. It was perfect. So I pulled it out and mounted the scope, putting a pellet in and setting my target at 40 yards. It was off to the right by two inches, so I turned the winding screw two clicks and repeated it a couple more times until I had it dead-on. It had to be, for what I wanted to accomplish.

As I arrived home, I casually grabbed the trash can from out of the trunk and strolled inside. In the past, my mom taught me "Patience, Paulie." It was a hard lesson throughout my years, but it helped me learn to understand.

Once inside, I took my sweet time. A couple of days passed by and I put some serious thought into what I wanted to achieve. Sooner than I expected, and a whole lot more powerful, a hurricane hit with winds of 50 miles per hours. My wish to Mother Nature had not been that severe.

So I decided to have some fun. I went up to the attic, opened one of the two windows, and loaded the gun repeatedly. I didn't use the scope. I just pointed and fired at least 80 times. I couldn't tell how much damage, if any, was being done; it was far too rainy to see.

The next day, it was sunny; the hurricane had moved on. I grabbed my video recorder and opened the window a couple of inches, zooming in to where I had aimed the pellet rifle. My eyes went wide and I almost dropped the camera for laughing so hard.

The box looked as if it had been hit by a shotgun shell. The wires hanging from the bottom had nicks in them; the box itself was not penetrated. At first, I had thought that the box was fiberglass, but I later understood it to be a carbon steel. Plus, the angle from whence I had been shooting didn't have a head-on shot to the telephone pole itself. I could see the pellets wedged in the construction, and I saw pieces of wood splinters.

I closed the window and headed downstairs to turn on my Camera Hunter. I could tell what frequency Fay was using. Like I said about the Hunter, it was perfect. Every time I turned it on in my apartment, in the corner of my living room, I got a strong reading-- and right outside, about 25 yards away, was that box.

I watched the news deep into the week, waiting for a weather report. As the meteorologist gave a seven-day update, I said to myself that Miss Nature was being very bad. A couple of days until thunder and lightning.

But I wanted to check something out first.

When I zoomed in on the wire hanging from the box, something didn't register, even with the rain and the wind. I had hit it at least five times in different spots, but I hadn't done much damage.

So I headed to this electronics store and asked the sales clerk about wiring my surveillance camera to my IP address. I also made it clear that the wire would be in a harsh environment. I just gave him some bullshit story. As he scrolled through different wire types, I was looking as well, and one word got my attention: "Kevlar." Specifically, Kevlar wrap stranded cable. I immediately stopped the dude from scrolling and asked for a printout. I shook his hand and asked for a business card; the least I could do was give him high hopes for a future sale.

I knew for what Kevlar was designed: bulletproof vests. It's not just the material. It's also the weave, the pattern that catches the bullet upon impact. In time, wearing it would loosen the weave, which makes the material less impact-absorbent.

In my situation, I had different intentions.

55

Back at home, I grabbed my drill and a two-inch-diameter drill bit. I had thought this out very well and headed to the attic. I laid on the floor, in a sniper position, and angled the drill.

"My boys' grandmom won't mind me putting a hole in her wall," I said as the drill pushed through. I could see my target.

The spot that I had chosen couldn't be seen by either camera.

Fay likely thought that I would take my pellet rifle and simply open a window, hang the barrel out, and shoot.

First of all, it was loud. The neighbors below me would have heard it plain as day. Secondly, I didn't want his video to capture anything, as it's recorded right onto a DVD.

The next day, midafternoon, she let loose. First the lightning, then the thunder. And the pellet was off to its target. I could see through the scope that it was a hit.

My intentions weren't to destroy the box, but to wound it. You have to understand me as a person: Once something is defeated, it would have to be replaced. If some dude came down to fix it or make some kind of adjustment, I would ask him what he was doing-- basically "play dumb" and put the dude on the spot.

I pushed down on the barrel, slipped another pellet in, and the crosshairs were on the second wire. Just like that, I could see it was a hit.

I took three more shots at each wire.

I was also curious about this CAT-5 optic cable. I knew my neighbors below me didn't have a computer, and the wiring itself looked new.

As I looked through the crosshairs, I whispered "Don't worry. I'll be right back." I grabbed my Camera Hunter and went to the living room to scroll to the R F band. That always gave a strong reading. The Hunter has a bar graph just like a cell phone, and, in that corner, it was at full bars all the time, even then.

I guess my shot didn't pierce enough.

I pushed the scroll up to the WiFi 2598-2602. That's where Fay's video was and still is.

I never could see the actual video of my apartment, but it showed an encryption he would periodically switch up to throw me off.

Sometimes it would show a low-budget religious movie; other times it would be just a stupid picture, or a web page.

Miss Nature was taming things down. So I headed back up, reloaded, and the crosshairs were on the targets once again.

This time, I concentrated on the spots that had already been hit. I was patient. Focus. I squeezed the trigger.

I only took five shots at the two wires. I cocked the rifle, eased the pellet in, and the CAT-5 cable was in my sights.

The wire looked to be only a quarter-inch in diameter versus the other two-and-a-half-inch wires.

As the shot was fired, Miss Nature skipped town.

"Oh well," I said. "I'll miss her."

As I got the cable lined up in the scope, I gave a dry lock, then pinned the hairs on. Next thing I know, Mr. CAT-5 was kinked; one more shot like that, and it would break.

I was pleased with my shots, but not yet satisfied.

Back in the living room with the Hunter on, I scrolled to the R F band. I just smile and was pleased. When I scrolled to the WiFi band, I was satisfied.

Ever since I moved in, the Hunter had always been five bars strong. Now, it displayed no bars. It just showed the little antenna icon, surrounded by a whole lot of blank space. What that adds up to is that, while the outside equipment was still functioning, it wasn't directing enough R F signal toward my apartment anymore.

The WiFi was still intact and showing its encryption.

I closed the screen door, living room window, and bedroom window. All three had a view of my target before I went to the attic. I cracked each window two inches just in case they would tempt Fay to focus on those areas.

I didn't leave it at that, either. Just like the linesman phone back at the Hut.

The next night, I was up in the attic with no weather to muffle the sound. But I'd take whatever makes a lot of noise.

The passenger trains came by every half-hour, and they were only 50 yards away.

My intentions were to make some sparks, some flashes. I knew the camera on the corner had a 360-degree view that included the box.

I didn't use pellets that time. Instead, I cut the tip off of six penny nails, being that the box was carbon steel and the impact of the nail would produce a good spark.

Waiting for my train to pass, I hear it just like I had a thousand other times. I moved the crosshairs to the face of the box. I saw a little flash. As I was laughing, the noise from the shot got my attention.

"That was loud," I mumbled.

Is it because the weather is calm, I thought, *or is it the ego effect?*

56

As I was sprawled out, gun loaded, waiting for my train, I was thinking I could make a silencer to reduce the noise. But, on the flipside, that's a federal offense.

The way I knew Fay, he'd find a way to make it a felony even though it was only being used for a pellet rifle. I didn't want to take any chances if this plan backfired on me. Besides, I only wanted to take a few more shots.

The other thing that crossed my mind: Don't think of me as some kind of rifleman. I got lucky with my shots, for what I had set out to do.

That said, I feel the right to bear arms should be legal. It started back in the caveman days. The way I see it, when man came out of the cave, he was "armed" with a club or a spear or whatever. He didn't know if there could have been a T-rex waiting to attack him and, on top of that, I am sure there weren't many cavewomen. He also didn't know if there was a cavedude trying to push up on his women.

Always defend yourself from what might be a threat.

"Finally," I whispered. The lights from the train, the right moment, and another good spark converged to mark the spot. I repeated it one more time, and my present be known.

Soon after, Fay was waiting for me. He knew about the two-inch sniper hole I had drilled. If you stood out in front of my place, you could see the hole. He was banking on the notion that I was going to finish the job. He knew I understood the encryption video on my Hunter. When my place is being triangulated, anything that works off of an R F signal-- he would get a reading of that. In his mind, the normal thing for me to do would be to destroy the video.

After three years going on four, I have more surveillance trained on me than any celebrity. It bothers me, but I learned to ignore it, and let me say that it wasn't easy.

A thought used to cross my mind. Let's say a couple of dudes had no inkling of the surveillance of my place and it's just a random burglary. I'm getting out of my car and the two dudes jump me. Fay's there and he sees this on his screen.

Another guy sitting next to him says, "Paulie just got hit by a two-by-four. Think we should call 911?"

"No," Fay replies. "No, he can handle himself." Meanwhile, I'm crawling on the ground.

About a week later, after my last shot had been fired, I got home from the gym and my neighbor approached me.

"Paulie," he said, "did you notice that hole up in your siding?"

"No," I replied. "It probably happened during the hurricane. Or it's old." *Just play dumb,* I thought.

"Yeah, we were looking at it through a pair of binoculars."

I just stood my ground and said that the winds must have been strong. I left it at that.

As I walked into my apartment, my mind was working. *Another neighbor coaxed into the bullshit.* I looked at the obvious. She was a 45-year-old hooker. She had a retarded kid in her apartment and the child wasn't hers. Fay saw the combination as an opportunity. That's how his mind works. Here's how it probably went down: He busted her for prostitution, then threatened her with child welfare services if she didn't cooperate.

Common sense said that the house was old. There were shingles missing from the roof on both sides and, if one were to look at the box, well... it looked like a shotgun had hit it. I knew damn well he was familiar with the box from our previous conversation and it's only human instinct if you're looking through a pair of binoculars; surely you'll focus on the box, especially when I elaborated about it. I was cultivating a sense of humor about it. The other neighbors at the Hut conveniently moved into a cheap apartment in a good neighborhood.

I'm not going to dwell on it. It is what it is.

57

    It was like putting an electronic puzzle together. Deciphering the different sound waves directed toward my apartment was not an easy task-- even for one who has experience with cellular technology.
    At the Hut, the 13-inch TV was the focus. I really didn't understand why... until now.
    The sound waves! They were interfering with the triangulation. So precautions had to have been put into effect. That's where the box, and the tunes I heard on the AM station, came into play.
    Don't ask me how I stumbled on the AM tunes. Naturally, everybody listens to FM, but, on that one day, I dialed it to 960... then I heard it. And I heard it pause for 12 seconds. And it repeated. But, as I backed away, it faded. The most intense reception was at the back of the house, about 2,000 yards away-- but you could see the cell tower as I did this. And I did it repeatedly, to make this claim. To make sure, I left the radio

tuned into that station for days when I was driving, and I never heard it.

A radio is a receiver. The difference between FM and AM is a lower band of frequency. Having said that, the radio is more vulnerable to deflections of signals or sound waves.

Fay didn't like it when I played Paul Revere, telling everybody. It made him look like a retard, and his technology a reject.

The only reason these two elements were needed, Fay knew, back at the Hut, I made an asshole out of him and his stooges. So he figures he'll be prepared and set up shop before I move in.

His objective on this topic is keeping the local channels in sync. If they aren't, it disorients the triangulation.

Back inside my apartment, I grabbed my receiver, attached my antenna to it, and plugged in my headphones. When using an audio receiver, upon turning it on, you'd expect to hear your local AM news station. But, when I tuned that out, I heard the signals.

When listening, I heard the distinctive tones and their patterns. Each R F band has its purpose. In cellular technology, phones work off of a certain band, with a certain frequency to define it. As for Fay's technology-- it's a bit similar, but a great deal more advanced than you could imagine. Understand that it was designed for the military and was later passed down to assorted government agencies.

With my headphones, I moved about, listening to the sounds as I swept the receiver, hoping the antenna would catch a magnetic deflection.

In the past, and in the present, Fay would use the strategy "Ghost."

What that means is that, when someone has surveillance on an individual, he sought for you to be paranoid or seeing "ghostly illusions." Previously, Fay would have had his confidential informants say "it's not him" or "he doesn't have the time" -- something of that nature.

In the beginning of 2008, Fay preprogrammed one of my cells with his initials. Why? Because he was a smartass who knew my sister has caller ID. I never thought it would get this far-- it was just another shovel of dirt, to go with the many others.

So, a month before Halloween, I bought a hanging ghost skeleton, bent its finger and thumb to resemble a gun, and hung it outside my entrance. From there on out, it became the Holy Ghost, and it stays there to this day.

The only things in which I believe are myself and the Man upstairs. Anything else is just a myth.

In the back of the house, I got the strongest signal in the left corner.

Besides my receiver, I would use my tape recorder, with the window glass amplifying the triangulation.

In sum: Two separate signals for the TV, three R F signals to triangulate, and the Wi-Fi out front and up the street. If those aren't enough, there's one more.

Before I moved into my apartment, I was only there one time, and I did a quick check with my Hunter. Nothing. Two months later, I moved in.

That gave Fay time to set up shop. He thought that would be check and mate. Like I've been saying, it's always been about getting his signal directed in. What he didn't count on was my Hunter and that I upgraded my antenna such that it received the signal from a greater distance.

Adjacent to my place, there are two streets-- the one in front, and the other, about 75 yards away, extending from the back. Fay had one of his cameras on the telephone pole. From my place, with the Hunter tuned in to a certain band channel, I could see the cars as plain as day. I also knew where, exactly, the camera was hidden... in a local cable box. You could see the silhouette in the background.

This particular camera always shows up on the Hunter. Never did I observe any others like this one. Once the Hunter tuned it in, it showed a strong reading; the triangulation picked it right up and Fay recalibrated the signal to its spot. He put some thought into that.

If you think this sounds like a clusterfuck, you'd be right. Now, let's dismantle that electronic puzzle.

Though millions of dollars' worth of technology are involved, Fay was bewildered that I could pick it apart so easily. It's one thing to detect signals, but to jam the entire technology?

That's major. I wouldn't be writing this if he didn't have this vendetta. Not only did I punk _him_ numerous times, but I did the same to his technology, as you'll read.

Whether it's data, video, or voice, the technology works on radio waves. Remember the pebble in the pond? So if I threw another stone from the other side, the ripples from both of them would clash and become disoriented.

I rigged the 13-inch TV to the telephone line and local cable service. Even though I didn't use a provider, it still existed, come from the previous tenant-- same for the landline, wherewith I used a combination of different splitters. Sometimes I would run the radio through them.

Back at the Hut, I used the cell phone booster. It was bizarre. Sometimes I could hear the TV buzzing for 10 minutes or so, then just stop. The noise was like being under a tower of power lines. I thought the TV was going to blow up, but it stood its ground, and continues to do so to this very day.

Imagine Fay sitting with another technician and they're both wearing headphones. Now, the other dude doesn't know me; he was sent over from the agency to oversee and correct what Fay fucked up. All of a sudden, the dude puts his hands his headphones, trying to zero in on what's being heard. At the same time, Fay is also listening, and he's familiar with my tactics.

The dude says, "What's that?"

"Spanish radio station," Fay replies.

Ten minutes later, a new sound.

"What's that?"

"Spanish TV station.

The dude takes off his headphones and says, "Is this individual a Latino?"

"No," Fay says.

The dude slowly puts on his headphones and looks at Fay as if to say "Boy, you really fucked this technology up." Fay just sits there, lost for words. Instead of his headphones, he wishes he had ear plugs.

I sent everything possible to disturb his signal. During all of this, I would place the tape recorder in the back of the house, leaning against the window, and gather the ringtones. These sounds are the motor switches in the computerized technology. Without going into deep detail, I'll leave it at that. Upon listening to the recording, you'll hear and understand how the ringtones are in sync with one another.

Until I start my "shove it up your ass technology," it's all over. Then you can actually hear the ringtones choking up and skipping. If you know what to listen for, you can hear Fay trying to adjust the system. When this is occurring, the data and cell frequency can't be retrieved.

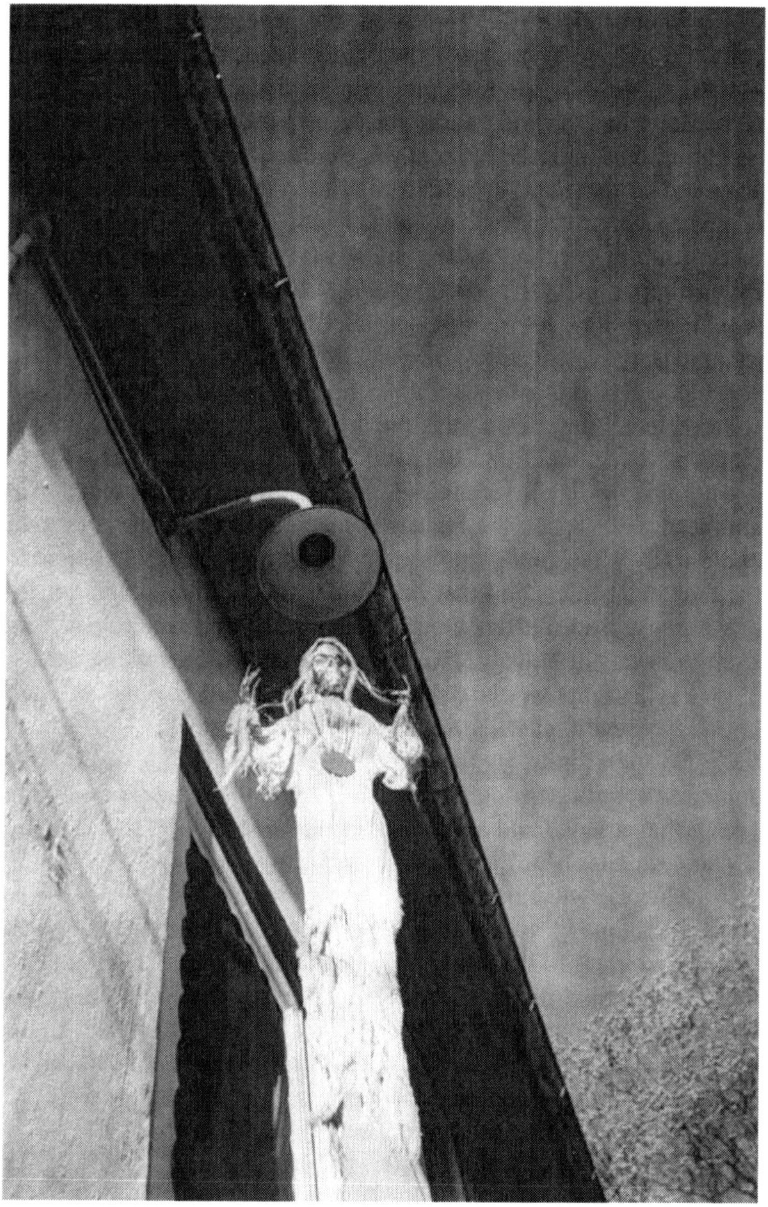

With the box working at 20%, Fay has options. He could have one of his stooges park a car and leave his cell phone on while another picks up... I've seen that at least 50 times. Or he could do a drive-by to see if the cell frequency is being retrieved properly. Just as an example-- say a dude in a car has laser technology and is doing surveillance on you. His objective is to point an invisible laser beam at the window; any sound or voice is absorbed by the glass, then transmitted to the beam and back to the receiver, where it gets demodulated into a voice or sound. But there's a thing called white noise that absorbs any unwanted eavesdropper in that particular area. Every once in a while, I would give Fay high hopes, think that he had corrected his triangulating system.

You'll find this hard to believe. This started in late 2008 and went on every day. Don't ask me how I did it-- what I do know is that it's November 28th, 2011, and this still goes on, and I still put a whippin' on Fay's technology. Even moreso, I'm taking it to another level. When the Hunter comes out to hunt, the prey will come. Fay's technology, especially in triangulation, is similar to the Hunter. Understand that the Hunter was not manufactured for this purpose. But it offers the same bands as Fay's technology, and from the years of bullshit, I've come to learn which ones he uses.

Fay's computerized technology is designed to retrieve a cell phone frequency. It will also show other R F signals.

Now, to bring in the prey, I turned on the 13-inch TV-- sometimes with the converter box, sometimes without. The Hunter has a video and audio jack on the side. I plug that into the TV or converter box, then a cable line of my choice.

Always switching it around.

Sometimes I would ground the cable to the radiator, which has cast iron ties to the meter and goes underground.

Understand that it's about electricity; somewhere along the line, it grounds out.

I scrolled the Hunter between 1850 MHz and 200 MHz. Some were more productive than others. I could tell by the nose produced and viewing the screen.

About 10 to 15 minutes later, the prey came.

Fay didn't know whether it's real. His equipment was getting a reading.

I'd be looking out the window, and there would be one of his stooges on his cell phone. My assessment of the situation? The stooge is in the Triangle and Fay is locked onto _his_ cell frequency, trying to determine or detect whether mine's legit.

Soon after the stooge left, I started it up again. Sometimes four o'clock in the morning.

Just to fuck with him.

58

There's an old saying-- "New Sheriff in town." I say "There's a new Hunter in town, and his name is Paulie."
    Now, it didn't stop at that. I discovered something with the landline that I didn't come to understand until later. I saw a local phone provider at a phone box about 40 yards from my place at least 12 times. It was one that was at ground level, three feet in height and two feet wide.
    I can't say I understand why.
    What I understood was my one receiver. It has a meter, meaning a needle that identifies magnetic deflection, and also a landline adapter to check for wiretaps.
    In the terminal's landline box, there are four wires: green, yellow, black, and red. I supposed that, with time and wear from my disconnecting the receiver, the red wire had detached from the screw.
    That's when I noticed that the needle didn't move, so I attached an alligator clip to the copper wire, and when I decided to shove it up his ass, that's when I connected the clip and the screw.

Like I said, I really didn't understand. I just knew that, over the duration of different, assorted times, the needle's activity decreased or increased when the dude was tinkering inside the phone box.

59

I had a gut feeling about the neighbors below me. Moreso she than he. When you see the same pattern and tactics time and time again, you come to understand. It was like a job and I had to beware of my surroundings.

A couple of days after I moved in, I engaged in small talk with the dude and gave him a briefing of what's been going on. Also, I gave him a partial draft of this very story, just as I'd given it to the others.

Now, her, she was doing her tricks. Like I said, getting all dolled up -- high heels -- the works. Late hours. One time, I saw a dude driving the neighbors' truck, with her hanging on to him as he was driving.

"Bimbo," I whispered to myself.

I never said anything to the guy downstairs. It's none of my business and I left it at that.

But Fay had found "a perfect stooge" for what he had in mind.

Bimbo was no longer doing tricks.

Part of Fay's surveillance program: He has drivers. They're not cops-- just stooges. Anyone from teenagers to adults of any fashion or from any forum.

Their sole purpose is to blend in. With their cell phones next to a person or residents and Fay focuses his technology on the stooge's R F... when that happens, it goes right into the Triangle.

Slick and scary.

Now, Bimbo has a so-called "job." I see her routine changes-- no heals or anything of that nature. Just going out to be a stooge. But not for long. Fay had other plans for her residence in mind.

Because Fay's technology is working half-assed, instead of sending a stooge to my surrounding area with his or her signal, Bimbo would just be used, talking on her cell. That way, he could somewhat keep it intact and tell what, if anything, was legit.

It sounds complex -- that it does -- but that's how it works.

The real gatekeeper here in the 13-inch TV. Here is the 13-inch TV. You may laugh, and so do I, but remember Mr. Wilson, back at the hut, staring at it is if it were some exotic dancer. And I mean it when I say "exotic." And the one time he was playing dumb when he was in the apartment above me for three hours right above the TV?

It would make you wonder.

60

"This is the tombstone!"

The local TV stations working through the digital converter box send very strong signals. If they're disoriented, it sends wave patterns, and that disrupts Fay's technology and the data that he's trying to receive.

When you look back, Fay put different methods on this particular issue, as you have read.

For me to elaborate on the fine details... I can't. It was so easy. No money was spent-- not a dime. Just common sense. Even a child could perform what I stumbled upon.

For me, I felt that it was earned, and I take it to my grave with that tombstone above me and a smirk on my face.

Remember, earlier in this story, I spoke about the earthquakes, asteroids, et cetera? It's all about waves. Shockwaves or soundwaves... it's all the same principal.

The technology is designed so that it can't be detected by a human being. We hear our sounds in "Decibels." There are a number of milestones: 30 Db would be a whisper; between 50 and 60 is a comfortable, conversational range; 70 is associated with vacuum cleaners and hair driers; 85 and up could cause loss of hearing.

Bats? Their hearing is unbelievable. They hunt and communicate by sound. If I were to blow into a dog whistle and tune it into their frequency, they would crash. How do I know that? From when I was a kid. Just being a boy.

The technical aspect of triangulation is not to be detected, so the receiver that's being used to detect and decode a certain R F. For that, it uses DBM. They come in an array of ranges... anywhere from 101 to one-fifteen. It depends on the cell tower, the terrain, the antenna type, et cetera.

Anyway, back to my story.

As the weeks turned into months, and I was distributing partial drafts of this story, as usual, and chatting with the recipients about certain details, I was also brewing a Witch's Punk recipe.

After five months, it was "potent."

In the beginning of this process, in late 2008, I was passing out parts of this story and would quote my paragraphs by saying that "you'll read what I want you to read." See what I want you to see. Hear what I want you to hear.

I guess Fay didn't take me seriously.

And you know the old saying... "Loose lips sink ships." And let me say that Fay sank an aircraft carrier.

In that five-month span, I was showing, telling, talking, pointing things out in a high-tech cellular technology magazine.

I wanted that Witch's Brew to be just right, so I added one more zesty spice.

So I copied about six pages out of that magazine and put it into the story. I claimed to intend on having them published in my book.

For the duration of these five months, Fay was telling his stooges, his peers -- anyone who would make himself look as if he's the main head honcho. Fay was overwhelmed by this, as I managed to punk him repeatedly... over 40 times.

Now, in his warped mind, he considered it a perfect opportunity to run Paulie into the ground.

Little did he know, those six pages never existed.

So, when this book comes out and the story is read, all of those stooges and peers will be laughing their asses off.

And that's how loose lips sunk the carrier, and the Witch's Brew came to a head, and a man got punked again.

61

    I like to say to people that I was tutored by a countersurveillance person, but it was just me and the Man upstairs.
    Let's take a ride down memory lane. When I purchased all of those cell phones and let you in as the Passenger, try to understand this so-called "investigation" on me. Almost five years and a whole lot of money spent. A lot of things and issues that don't add up. I also want you to picture yourself in an "electronic surveillance maze" and, let me warn you, one slip and it's game over. So let's take that ride.
    Whenever I left the Hut, a video and motion sensor sent a text or SMS alert back to Fay. I was on my way to purchase a cell. Also, I was being tracked by IP and WiFi cameras and stooges.
    But let's say I ducked him and took a side road. I'd still have to come onto a main street and the camera would view me exiting, beginning the tracking again.
    Let's drive a little faster on this topic.

Say I evade him that day or evening. I still have to come home sooner or later. But what happens is that, when I trip the motion sensor, it sends the message.

And this is the part that Fay doesn't like for some reason.

Whatever camera it may be, always recording, if Fay thought it would be necessary, he would have a surveillance person backtrack my driving.

With this type of technology, and with a DVD recorder, it doesn't take long. That's the sole purpose for the motion sensor alert.

Maybe I pulled a fast one on Fay by purchasing my cell phone. Or maybe I didn't.

Now it gets tricky.

For the obvious reasons, timeframe and cell towers, backtracking took place. It revealed that I was at a nearby outlet store a couple of towns away. With the technology in front of him, it can be programmed to show any new cell phone being activated. What happens is that the closest tower to the outlet is used for the activation of a cell phone. Fay narrowed down the timeframe that I was in there and started his search.

When a new cell is programmed or activated, you receive a courtesy message and a phone number. That's for what he's looking. For if there are 20 activations, he'll check each one. He has a few options in his checking process.

Now, understand that I was back home, in the Triangle. I couldn't leave the cell on-- that would just be stupid. So I kept it off.

Fay's checking process could be done by calling the cell number and seeing whether someone responds or sends a text message, and then see whether the person read it. If there's no response either way, that will raise a red flag. It's only natural that, when you buy a new cell phone, you'll keep it on and open any messages that come through.

For the first six months, Fay had my cell phone number. I couldn't understand how, but then I caught on. He enjoyed playing games with me, sending me corny text messages like "Do you swallow," "Identify yourself," "I'll shoot you in the fuckin' head," and one even read "Somebody be upstairs." At the Hut, I resided in the finished basement. Sometimes I would be leaving the gym and a text would appear that simply said "Hi."

The on things I can say about that? Corny and gay.

He dishes it out and I dish it right back.

My dish was more of a statement. One evening, it rained. I knew Fay was onto this one cell I had. He was waiting for me to use it. I guess he thought that I'd called somebody important.

That I did.

The rain stopped and I went to this river where Zorro enjoyed playing. He wasn't a good swimmer; he just liked trading water, having fun with his dad.

I turned the cell on and texted a message to a state representative. It read, "Need to talk A.S.A.P." I punched in the number, pushed send, slid the phone into a plastic bag, dropped in a protein container, screwed the lid back on, and chucked the package into the river. I saw that it was moving at a pretty good pace.

"That's for my son, motherfucker," I said on the walk back to the car.

The idea behind this was to give Fay somebody important, and I wanted to keep that cell drifting at a good pace. Why? Because, as it's moving along, it's being tracked by the technology and cell towers.

I didn't want the cell phone to be retrieved. The river was my transporter. Fay would sit, trying to triangulate the cell, but he couldn't understand how it was being moved. That's a statement... and another "Punk" to add to the list.

So we got back into the car with the new cell, halfway through that electronic maze.

As we left, the motion sensor was tripped. The both of us chose a fine restaurant to eat on the way. The receivers hanging from the streetlights were scattered randomly, so it wasn't safe to turn on the cell just yet.

We got to our fine dining place, but we were also tracked. We sat at the bar because of how busy the restaurant was. Fifteen minutes later, a couple of stooges sat themselves right next to us, trying to blend in with their cell phones. We finished eating and having our couple of drinks. Time to go.

One of the stooges informed Fay that we were leaving and had showed no signs of using a cell phone.

It was dark. Father time had set in, and my Passenger was feeling stressed out.

I took the person to their car and gave a polite smile and the sentiment that "Tomorrow is another day."

The infrared on the cameras and the blue light were of no help to me. The cameras could see just as well at night time, and the blue light on my cell was a dead giveaway. I knew Fay was focusing on that. It was to his advantage.

But I had an important call to make. I also had to be aware of my voice pattern. If Fay knew my area, he could have programmed the technology to that tower for a voice analysis. It's just like a fingerprint.

So I decided to do it the safe way... texting. I sent four messages and four replies came back. One of the messages read "Check out the cameras on 202 South and the north lanes on the cement bridge." There was a smiley emoticon attached to the end.

I had known this person for many years. His sarcastic thinking and tendency to be a ballbuster reminds me a lot of myself.

So I decided to check it out. I knew there was more to the picture.

I was familiar with this highway, as it led away from King of Prussia Mall. The cement bridge was just a ways up the road, and I saw what my boy was getting at.

The camera was pointing at a downward angle, just slightly, in a positioned way. I drove towards it and got off at the exit to make my way southbound. As I was approaching the bridge, I pulled onto the shoulder and simply thought.

I texted my boy "He's a sick individual" and the reply that came back was "You got that right."

You, the reader? I want you to have an open mind and use good common sense with regard to this ordeal.

I'm not suggesting that those cameras were meant for me, but, in the past and present, it's become clear that Fay likes to watch and listen. I also knew that this person used the technology for his own personal needs, such as his wife.

I came to understand his warped mind, and how he uses the job that represents law enforcement, citizens of the community, and most of the technology.

Remember... common sense!

Let's say it's a quiet evening. You're driving with your girl and she's feeling a little desire to please you, so she gets into position and leans over, and the cruise begins with the sun roof open.

You're enjoying the moment. You see lights flashing ahead of traffic. It's bumper to bumper and, ultimately, it comes to a stop. You look up through the sun roof and see a camera looking straight down onto you. Do you stop your girl from bobbing up and down or does "Why would it be at that angle?" cross your mind?

Now let's say that there's no traffic at all. You're cruising at 50 MPH. How many bobs could Fay see? Just one?

Maybe, with Fay, that's all he needs to satisfy his pleasure.

The evening was just about to come to an end. You both enjoyed your favorite restaurant, belly full and balls empty, but the curious mind wonders.

Now, the way I see and view the situation: In the town in which I live, never did I see a camera pointed in that position, and let me say that there are at least a hundred or so of traffic lights that are angled or slanted to look ahead. I can't even give the benefit of the doubt that it's for viewing a license plate. That angle would not capture a plate number.

Here's a possibility-- Windows tinted, it's dark, the sun roof is open, and the blue light from the cell was visible.

If that was the case, then there would be such others in the town. Fay knows that, if a man were to get a blow job and enjoy it, it's going to be on a stretch of highway without stop-and-go traffic. Just a smooth ride.

For this, I christen Fay "Thrill Seeker." A.K.A., "Peeping Tom."

You, as a reader, should always use caution when performing this act. Say a deer ran out in front of your vehicle. The impact alone could be severe. And I, as a pedestrian, see the collision and come running over to assist with the situation, only to find your girl's head pinned beneath the steering wheel.

Me, being a simple-minded dude, would probably just comment "Obviously, you didn't read my book!"

I headed home for the night, knowing that my Passenger was in for a rough ride.

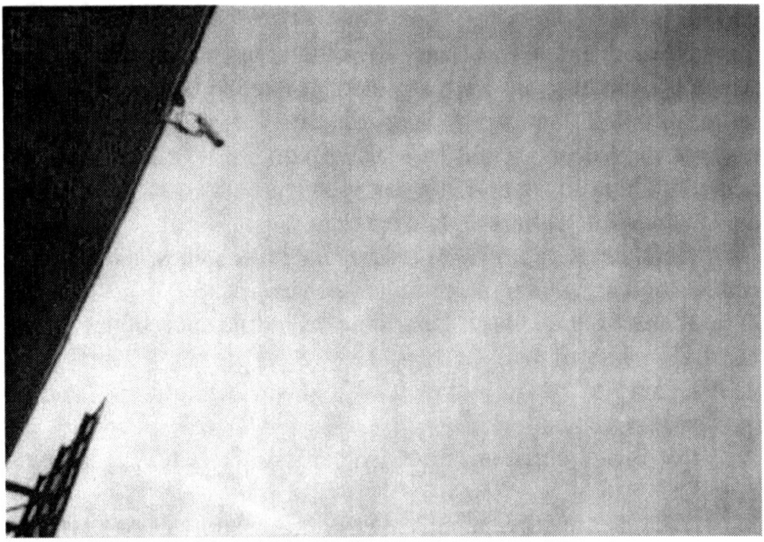

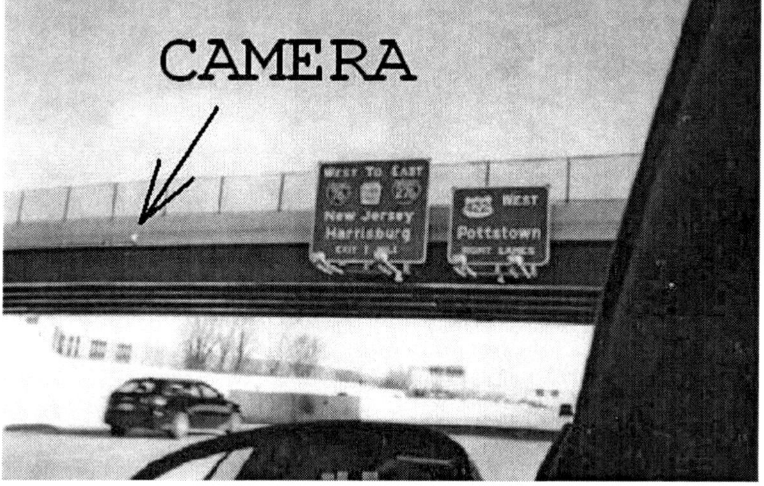
CAMERA
New Jersey
Harrisburg
WEST
Pottstown

62

That morning, Cheerios, as always, and I'm on my way. I glanced upward at the telephone pole in front of my apartment and the streetlight is on, even though it's daylight. Just like the old people next to the Hut, when they couldn't understand why the light was coming on, even during the day.

The simple, logical reason is magnetic deflection from the electricity triggering the motion sensor.

The bottom line is that Thrill Seeker's R F signal is sweeping the telephone pole.

As I was backing out into the street, I looked down the road and up at the other streetlights-- and they're not on. I just shook my head. I guess I'm just that acquainted with it.

I'm not saying that every streetlight on during the day in that particular area is being triangulated. Understand that there are a lot of drawbacks about the technology.

More than likely, the time table lets you notice you've been had! "My situation is completely different from any investigation anybody's ever heard of. Remember that."

As I was pulling up to our meeting spot, my Passenger slowly opened the door to get in. I sense that they feel it's the electric chair. I gave a laugh and a smile.

"You'll be fine," I said. "Trust me!"

As we made our way through that electronic maze, the tactics just got more devious.

My Passenger asked me if they could call their mother. "Yes and no," I start to explain.

Let's say I was on the FBI's Most Wanted List and I were to go to their website and cross-reference the name Paul Swist, remembering every computer has an IP address. By searching for my name, it would send an alert or a hit. The FBI has G-Men and G-Geeks that merely sit there, waiting, for that one possible lead to an arrest.

The curios mind of a criminal could be their faith.

I elaborated to my Passenger my reasoning of this scenario. In this day and age, the technology is four times more advanced compares to its state in the seventies and eighties.

Thrill Seeker knows that I'm very close to my mother, and, in the past, during our conversations, he would deliberately disconnect the call. Thinking that I'd used another cell, well... that happened one too many times. Thrill Seeker knows my mom's birthday and holidays, and he knows a son will call his mother.

It's the same format as the FBI Most Wanted List. Landline or cell phone, it doesn't matter. And my mom has no clue that her phone is being monitored or wiretapped.

My Passenger and I drove to the gym for our workout. After we were greeted, I asked to use the phone. And the dude placed the landline on the counter.

It was then when I said to my Passenger, "Now you can call your mom."

63

    Six months into this, I caught on to Thrill Seeker's ways. As I bounced around from gym to gym, they became acquainted with my strategy of using their phones. And I, as a people person, have explained details to some and gave portions of this story to others.
    As we exited, the cars were blanketed with snow and ice. My Passenger glanced over at me and said "Good or bad?"
    "You're catching on," I replied, "and I like that. Always be aware of your surroundings; you never know what could be looking at you.
    As the defroster melted the ice on the windshield, I told my Passenger about one incident wherein my girlfriend and I went to a jewelry story in this one town. As we were just about to exit the vehicle, I said to my girl, "Don't look, but there's a dude in the hallway off to the right. Tuck your arm around your pocketbook and walk casually." I got out of the car and instantly the dude noticed my size (or he knew that he'd been made) and he simply faded back into the hallway.
    "Did you bait your girl?" asked my Passenger.

"Maybe a little bit, but she understood me and my ways, and she knew that if I wanted that dude I'd have made an example out of him, if you know what I mean."

"You aren't right, Paulie."

"That's what they say!"

The ice had melted and it was time to move on.

As Jack Frost whitened the area, I explained to my Passenger the advantages and disadvantage of his presence. As the wiper blades were swishing the snow and ice, I pointed at several cameras that were on and mounted to the traffic lights. Some were shaped like a narrow shaving cream canister; others were more rectangular. Those are the ones that have heaters, in case Jack layers the outer lens with ice. Those are not cheap.

For Thrill Seeker, the cameras were tucked away from the elements. He likes using the local cable provider's box-- this way, the pinhole video camera is flush against the box. You'd never see it, but freezing rain will take its toll on it, and the seeker just can't see.

"What's so funny?" I ask my passenger.

"Every time you say 'Thrill Seeker,' it's hysterical, Paulie!"

"What can I say? He earned it." When a Mafia guy is accepted into the organization of the Family, he will usually inherit a nickname. For his character, for whatever it may be. For Thrill Seeker, he definitely earned it. I can't emphasize a better perspective than that and for me to shed more light on this, he's the one who introduced Fay into this story.

Maybe he's a cross-dresser... who knows? I just kept tabs on the issues that were directed at me.

64

I asked my Passenger to join me for lunch -- my treat -- and the offer was accepted.

As we were seated and looking at our menus, I glanced up and saw a stooge, but I don't say anything to my Passenger. I chose to play it out for the right moment.

I've been accustomed to that they weren't the brightest bulbs in the box. Sometimes, I saw "the real deal," meaning a dude with a badge trying to be slick. I'm no rookie-- even though I know that I'm not breaking the law, I understand individuals and their body language. The stooges are getting paid 10 dollars an hour. They're your average, everyday person. They come in all ethnicities. Race is not a factor. Because Thrill Seeker was wall-known, he could ask a favor of someone. There are so many possibilities, you couldn't imagine it. From truck and cab drivers to construction workers. I saw it all over the duration.

The way it works -- and Thrill Seeker was very, very persuasive -- a person's name works if he or she does the simple favor of just sitting in a car with his cell.

What I am getting at is that one deed deserves another. A traffic ticket, a DUI, et cetera. You never know. But you get my drift. That's the way it works.

As my Passenger laid the menu down, I gave a stare and said, "What did I say when I picked you up earlier, a phrase in a whisper? I said, 'trust me and you'll be fine.'" And I knotted my head and added "Don't look now, but there's a stooge."

The diner that I had chosen was a laid-back, good-old Pennsylvania Dutch Cooking establishment. Nothing fancy, and no dome cameras of any kind. Thrill Seeker has a habit (and the technology) to hack right in to any business that has IP video surveillance.

As I noticed the stooge holding his camera phone and pointing it at us, I said to my passenger, "Look at the dude to my right and just move your lips as if you're saying 'You got punked again.'" Good ol' Paulie, laughing as usual. It was just another day for me.

I gave my Passenger a wink and a smile, commending the first punk.

65

We finished our lunch back in the car. My Passenger asked me whether I had known.

"Yes," I said. "You know the line from that movie... 'if you build it, they will come.'"

Thrill Seeker knew there had been no IP camera through which to view. He knew his stooges weren't that bright. In his mind, I guess he thought that I might have been doing some lawbreaking.

I told my Passenger about this one time during which I was at a luncheonette. It seated only 15 people. As I was eating my sandwich, a stooge in his early 20s with mirrored glasses tripped right in front of my table. Almost landed right on top.

Me being me, I just laughed and said, "Those glasses are very shiny!"

I told my Passenger that it takes a special person to be cool and collect himself. You don't just run; you pace yourself so you don't trip like the stooge did.

My Passenger asked me the multi-million-dollar question. What could justify an investigation of this magnitude?

Eventually, there must have been some probable cause-- way too many people were aware that it was out in the open and questions kept being asked. Over four years and counting. It was not your typical investigation, nor was it tight-lipped.

My personal opinion? The Man upstairs chose me to bring the truth to the public and let it be known. Just as with bad priests, coaches, and pathetic Detectives, the dirt will come out sooner or later. The Man above me took some of my strength, meaning my boy Zorro; He knew I was devastated by his passing; He also was aware that I wanted to take someone's life. Revenge in His ways, it's not. Except, over time, I proved to myself to be a righteous person, and He gave me my strength.

Let me inject some realism into reality. You have state-of-the-art technology. It doesn't get any better than that over four years. If the Man upstairs wanted that Detective to direct the R F signal without any hassles, it would have been done.

Knowing that he abuses the technology for his own purposes, the man basically made an example out of himself. Shove it up his ass.

You ask me, and others have, too. Same question. I put it in black-and-white, other than that I have no answer. I gave my Passenger a glassy-eyed stare of sincerity.

"Can I ask you one more question?"

"You may," I replied.

"That picture on your arm-- is that in memory of Zorro?"

When it came to my boy, he'll never be forgotten. In the mid-80s, I purchased a Rottie. His name was also Zorro. He was a big boy... 185 pounds. Then I met a chick in whom we shared a mutual attraction. I told her to find an apartment in the King of Prussia area and she said that she had one: a Penthouse at the Valley Forge Towers. But pets weren't allowed. My brother and I, a true dog person, accepted him into our family and cherished him until his final days.

After I finished my Federal sentence, with my 15-year relationship with my girlfriend, we purchased a Rottie puppy, nine weeks old. He was our pride and joy. We separated and went our own ways. The only thing I wanted out of the relationship was Zorro. It got ugly between us, but I managed. He was my everything. We're in the very beginning of 2012 and there isn't a day that goes by when I don't think about him... and, most of all, what was inflicted because of a person's vendetta towards me.

And let me say that, throughout the duration of the years that went by, I probably asked at least 300 people, including law enforcement. If I made an accusation that you threw acid and poison at my dog, would you confront me? And they all said that they would.

I can't call him Thrill Seeker. It's way beyond that. It's just immoral. Either he did it, or he knows who did. End of story.

66

My Passenger got out of the car and lit a cigarette. I notice that each drag and each exhalation are done with intensity.

As the car door opened, I muttered, "You don't have to explain yourself." I also sensed that there was more to that curious mind.

"Let me pave it out for you!"

It's called "control manipulation." When these two words are combined, the result if the way I have been compared and seen over the years.

In the early 80s, there was a cult leader named Jim Jones. For one reason or another, he brainwashed his followers into drinking a Kool-Aid cocktail of poison... including the children.

Mr. Jones only cared about himself and his beliefs, whatever they might have been.

As for Thrill Seeker, he made a comment to me in 2008 that he has 450 people under him... who were they going to believe, him or me?

Those were his words, and I responded, "You're right."

As the time and bullshit went on, I've become aware of his tactics... using people, including law enforcement, whomever and whatever. It didn't matter.

Jim Jones could have spared those children, but he didn't. Thrill Seeker could have spared my boy, Zorro... but he didn't.

When the story is read, it paves a perfect road of control and manipulation.

As I stared out through the windshield and glanced over to my Passenger, I said, "It's getting late. Tomorrow starts with a new adventure."

"What do you mean by 'new adventure,'" says the passenger as the car doors open.

"You'll see! Get a good night's rest."

"That smirk! It's a killer, Paulie!"

Again, I say, "Get some rest."

67

    Back to the apartment to put my thoughts into place, and to seek out an editor for my book. Little did I know that I was in for a world of my own awakening.
    With Thrill Seeker up my ass and keeping a tab on me, he knows I have one and only one goal: to get my book published.
    I cannot emphasize this enough. He does not want this to be published into a book form by any means.
    Put yourself in his shoes, would you?
    Over the duration of this entire spectacle, I've learned about cellular technology, countersurveillance, representing myself in a courtroom, being my own lawyer, and becoming a writer... but I don't have the skills to proofread and put the material into an actual book format. Besides, I'm not looking for a publisher who could take years.
    At this point, just an editor. Real simple, you'd think.
    Over the course of a years' time, I went through at least 30 people and I met all kinds. With me having a short fuse, I bit my

tongue and just swallowed some of my dignity to move on to another person, but some things just didn't add up.

I even had a sit-down talk with my brother and showed him the different response letters I've gotten back from individuals. He says that maybe they didn't like the story and I say that I'm not in it for their opinion. I just want it cleaned up and edited into a book.

I understand my brother and his thoughts. He knows these episodes are out-of-the-ordinary, with him being a family man with a wife of kids-- it's just too deep. I've come to accept that as his brother.

Morning Cheerios as always, and I was going to meet my Passenger. As I arrived, the car door opens, and a voice speaks: "Turn your cell on, Paulie." There was a text message and it read "I got a good night rest."

I knew my Passenger wanted to impress me. (By the way, even if your cell is OFF, you'll receive the message regardless.)

I played along, asking, "Where did you learn that?"

"When I was cheating on my boyfriend and didn't want to acknowledge it to him until later."

I smile with this reply: "Simple-minded people like me," and we drove off to seek out an editor.

As I'm driving, I get asked how much it costs for someone to edit. I am willing to give him or her $1,500, and that's being generous.

I start to elaborate about different approaches and events that occur. But this one really stands out.

I'm in the deli area of this one grocery store. As I am waiting, there's this female next to me... blonde hair, in her late 30s. With me being a people person, and still in need of an editor, I inquire, and she reveals that her boyfriend is a skilled writer. She asks me what the story revolved around.

"Cellular technology and a dirty Detective using it for his own purpose."

I see her eyes open and she becomes more and more interested as I pile on the detail. Ultimately, she interrupts, and says that her boyfriend used to be a Detective.

Now, my eyes open even wider, and I asked her where.

"Lower Origin Township."

"What's his name?"

When she blurts it out, I developed a smile a mile wide, and say that there is a God looking over me.

She begins to tell me about this incident wherein S.W.A.T. came into their house, brandishing rifles, lasers, the whole nine yards, then cuff her boyfriend, who was subsequently locked up for two months in the county jail. I could tell that she had some bitterness reserved for law enforcement.

As she's expressing her emotions, I say "Let me have a number where I can get in touch with you," and she digs into her purse and gives me a business card that identifies her as a Realtor and provides her picture. I tuck it into my sweats.

"I'll be in touch in a couple days." And, with that, we part ways.

As I'm putting my groceries into my car, I see her from a distance, doing the same, but she's holding her hand up, as if talking on a cell phone, looking at me, making sure I call. I just give a smile and nod.

During our conversation, good and bad went through my mind. The good was that her boyfriend used to be a Narcotics Officer for the county many years prior. He knows me, but late, he came to work for Lower Origin Township as a Detective. From there on out, there must have been bad blood... especially if it had led to his getting locked up.

The way I see it, the girl and her boyfriend have their _own_ vendetta, and Paulie has his editor. A very knowledgeable one. Pluses across the board, you would think.

Now for the bad. Thrill Seeker, keeping tabs on me, knowing I'm looking for an editor. He's going to put a halt on the situation. What had I hadn't been aware of was the presence of a dome camera right above us in the deli.

"That was bad."

I've learned, seen, and experienced the things of which Thrill Seeker is capable. But I'm not going to judge anything just yet. I'll play it out.

68

I waited two days and placed my cell from a gas station. Her cell phone rang and went through to voice mail, but I didn't leave any message-- I simply thanked the guy for letting me use his landline.

I waited a couple hours and went to another station. Some response, and again, I left no message.

As I was explaining to my Passenger, I've experienced a carbon copy of this episode with a female I had met at a bar.

Later that evening, another station... and no response. Same old song. I had that gut feeling, and I was right, for the reasons of common sense.

Knowing she was a Realtor, her cell is _always_ going to be by her side. A call coming in could be an interested purchaser. That's money, plain and simple.

"I got you now, motherfucker," I say.

Never underestimate Paulie. I will do the unthinkable.

By her giving me the business card, that was my "ace in the hole." Information on the card led me to a real estate company, about a 15 minutes' drive away.

As I was greeted by the receptionist, I began to say that I wasn't there to purchase real estate, but I had met this lady at a grocery store. She had informed me that her boyfriend could be interested in doing some editing work. I show the receptionist the business card, and she recognized it. I mentioned that I made three different calls at various times, but there'd been no answer. I asked her whether that's odd.

"Yes!"

So the receptionist tried to call the number, but there was no answer. She then said that she would send her an e-mail informing her of my impromptu visit. I was asked for a contact number, but gave none. I said I'd be back the following day, and left it at that.

The next day, back I went, only to be told that there had been no response via either e-mail or cell phone. I thanked the receptionist for going out of her way.

Now that my I's were dotted and my T's were crossed...

69

Next phase: Lower Origin Police.
My passenger is laughing. "You ain't right, Paulie."
"That's what they say."
I went through those doors again, looking to see who's behind the glass. It isn't as if they don't know me. Because they _do_ know who I am.
"How may I help you?"
"I'd like to file a missing persons report." As I give a brief description, I also know that Thrill Seeker is well aware.
As I'm waiting for an Officer, 20 minutes lapse. I can only imagine what's going to come of this.
Soon after, a Patrolman exits out of the door and I explain to him how I had met this female. My voice, in general, is deep; when speaking, I let my presence be known. I tell him that I'm writing a book and that the missing person had informed me that her boyfriend was a Lower Origin Detective with editing skills. I see the Patrolman's eyes roll and the eyes behind the glass are viewing our conversation.

Doesn't take much to understand somebody's body language. He had already been briefed by someone else: Thrill Seeker.

I pass the business card to him and he says he'll try calling her.

I say, sarcastically, "_This_ should be good."

Three minutes later, the Patrolman comes back and says that he talked to her and she is terrified of me.

"You have got to be kidding. That's bullshit. You and I know it. That's bullshit and you and I know it!"

He looks at me and mentions that, if I go near her, I'll be arrested.

"Bullshit!"

I take the business card and go back to the glass to make an appointment with the Chief. It was set for the next day.

This was not what I had had in mind, but I wanted the Chief to know that his officers are being used for someone's bullshit.

The next day. You know the drill. Bust open the doors. Up to the glass. Announce my name.

A couple of minutes later, Don comes out, handshake as always, and your general how-you-doings. We head back to the room where we had had our previous sit-downs and I tell him what had occurred. He understands me very well. I know that nothing is going to come to this. On the other hand, he knew that I'd stuck it up Thrill Seeker's ass big-time.

Deeper into the conversation, I express my thoughts on Thrill Seeker. I assure him that there's no need to explain.

"You know within yourself the truth," I say. "That's all that matters now."

I change the subject of conversation shortly thereafter. We shake hands and I go home again.

P.S.: Don, I know you're reading this, and I can see the smile on your face. Good luck on your retirement and working out. Paulie

My Passenger asks me whether I really like the chief.

"Yes, he's an old-school person," I assure. "Nothing flashy. Just keeping it real..."

70

As the search goes on, I mention a few others. One day, I decide to go to this upscale beautician in an upper-class place. The notion that enters my mind is that it's Gossip City. Everybody knows other people's business. As I enter with my story intact, I go right to the receptionist and ask as to whether she knows anybody that happens to be an editor. At the same time, I mention my name and place my story on the counter, quoting that he or she would be paid $1,500 for their time.

As I mention this tale, there's an older lady -- mid-50s -- right beside me, and she's listening in.

"Young man," she speaks up, "young man. You don't come into an established business requiring an editor. I, myself, am an editor.

"Young man, come sit with me and tell me in 30 seconds why I have need to write this story."

As I am explaining, she grabs through the story and whisks through the pages. I'm looking at her, like, _you can't be for real._

She then tells me about the six languages she speaks.

Like I really give a fuck, I think.

Again, she says, "Young man, I'm also a psychologist."

What the fuck do you want, a trophy?

But I just keep my mouth shut. I basically allow her to run me into the ground as strangers listened in. I just grab my story, look at her, and conclude that "upper-class" has overwhelmed her soul.

I resolve, as I'm getting into my car, that, when this is published, I will take a copy to that place and say my piece.

My Passenger is laughing, "Paulie, Paulie...," and I say that there are all kinds out there, but if you don't ask, you'll never know.

71

I get some suggestions.
Did I try colleges? They have writing departments. Yes, I pursue a couple of them, but it's always bad timing, or they had their own work to be done. I even go to at least six nearly libraries.
Maybe it just wasn't meant to be. Or, simply bad luck. Sometimes I felt as if I was searching for Bigfoot or the Loch Ness monster and getting nowhere.
Other people that I meet think they could be of utility, so I pass a partial draft of the story and, a week later, they never meet me at the agreed-upon location. Or they just don't have the time. It's one thing after another.
I know that this story is meant to be. As you know, I am a firm believer of the Man upstairs. Yes, it's stressful -- all of the bullshit -- it makes you or breaks you and I didn't intend on the latter happening to me.
My mom always said: "See the signs. They will guide you through life. The destiny I choose will be mine to keep."

This one day, I approach another library. As I am talking to some individuals, I see this dude -- late 20s -- shy-looking. I can tell he's listening, but also feeling a bit intimidated by my presence, but what really catches my eye is that he has a short-sleeve shirt and a _Triangle_ tattoo on his right wrist that stands out to me. That's the only one I've ever seen. So, I go over to introduce myself, we discuss his background, and I give him a portion of the story and tell him how much I will pay.

A week later, I meet up with him and he says he'll do it.

I whisper to myself, "Thank you, Mom."

72

My Passenger is happy for me, but I can tell that more questions are surfacing.

"Do you think there is a conspiracy directed at you?"

"No! ...'Conspire,' *yes!*" The difference between these two are that, in a conspiracy, each individual would have to know who's doing what, and that wasn't the situation.

Conspire, by all means. Landlord, Probation Officer... the list goes on.

"Favor" comes into play. This is how it works: Say it's a late night. A law enforcement officer is stopped for speeding. Obviously, the cop will not write out a ticket.

On the other hand, if the officer is drinking one too many and wraps his car around a telephone pole, the cop has no choice but to write a ticket and file a police report.

As the story draws to the end for Thrill Seeker, the epitome resides in an "hourglass" with stooges, technology, tactics, and favors. Trickling to the bottom, time has run out. He can't flip it over. The sand is gone.

Where? Into my story, for my readers to see how one man backed up by millions of dollars of technology and manpower was defeated.

"A statement was made, and a long time to follow."
"Well said, Paulie."
"My female curious mind wonders... if I may."
"Go ahead!"
"Your love life."
"What about it?"
"Is there anybody?"
"No!"
"Think about it," I say. "If I meet a female and there's an attraction between us, the next step would be telling her about myself. How do I explain it? Let's say she just wanted to get laid. Knowing about Thrill Seeker and his videos, it just wouldn't be right."
"What about me, Paulie?"
"As you know, I call it as I see it. When I met you earlier today, you opened the car door and just stood there. The only things I saw were tan legs and a short skirt, and I smelled the aroma of perfume. The thought crossed the hell of seeking an editor."
"Good answer. What do you find in a female to be appealing?"
"Teeth," I reply. "My mom always said 'Look at them: They will tell you about her well-being, how she carries herself.'"
"Moms know, don't they, Paulie?"
"Yes, they do. If you're wondering, yes, they pass with flying colors."
"Thanks."
"Well, Paulie, it's getting late. You can take me back to my car, _or_ we can go back to your place and Thrill Seeker can get his thrills off."
"I _am_ a wild one," I smile.
"I plan on taming you down. That smirk? It's killer."
"I know."

I would like to end this story for you. As you know, there's a beginning, a middle, and an end. Unfortunately, I am still, to this very day -- February 20th, 2012 -- subjected to the same bullshit. I'm merely the writer, reporting on what happened.

But I leave this tale for a curious mind.

Thanx,
Paulie

EPILOGUE

With all of that said and done, there's an old parable left to be told.

And it goes like this: There were three guys. You would think that they were brothers. They had families and lived in a middle-class neighborhood. Jack, Steve, and Paul would only mingle amongst themselves.

Each week, they would have a bonfire at a different house. The wives would chit-chat and the kids would just be kids.

This one night, as they were sitting, drinking their bottles of beer, Steve leaned up on his chair, stared directly at the fire, and mentioned something about a bank heist. Next thing you know, Paul and Jack are on the edge of their seats, listing and giving input into the caper. It was as if they were all on the same wavelength.

They talked into the wee hours of the night. The wives had left earlier with the kids.

As for Jack's occupation, he was part-owner of a mining company. Steve's work was in manufacturing human prosthetics, and Paul had his own business designing and fabricating automotives.

This was not going to be some spontaneous bank job, but very well thought-out. They also knew the outcome would be devastating.

Five months into their caper, they were ready to rock 'n' roll. On their way, they didn't say a word to one another. Each of them Scotch-taped their fingers and passed the compact mirrors. They were totally amazed at how real the prosthetic gave that natural look.

They parked the car in a particular spot, just as they had with the other two on the night prior.

They entered the bank just like every other pedestrian. At the same time, all three voices barked out to get down and stay down. Paul and Jack gathered the money and Steve watched over the customers and tellers. There was a lot of cash.

They were in no hurry. They also knew that the silent alarm had been activated. Soon after, Jack gave a nod to Paul and Steve then glanced out the window. There were marked police cars and a visible S.W.A.T. truck.

They got what they came for!

And now everybody was directed to the front entrance and ordered not to turn around. Jack, Steve, and Paul pulled their cell phones out and turned them on. Paul dialed a number and the other two followed suit.

The next things that were heard were three explosions. It sounded like a combination of an F5 tornado and a freight train. Glass flew everywhere. One could see the bodies of uniformed police officers being lifted from the ground. People started to run out of the bank. It was chaos!

The three of them unzipped their jumpsuits and blended into the crowd with their briefcases before disappearing.

Many weeks afterward, it was broadcast all over the news. Always, the headlines read "Three Caucasian males are wanted for killing 125 and critically injuring another hundred."

A while after things started to calm down, Jack, Paul, and Steve distanced themselves, but not completely.

Each of them thought about his involvement. Jack, part-owner of a mining company, had access to C4 explosive; Paul fabricated cars and built them from scratch, leaving no identifying numbers to match or trace; Steve manufactured the prosthetics used to perfectly alter their appearances. And any video that may have been captured in the bank or from the street was useless.

The money changed their lives. There was no happiness. Just regret and misery.

Steve bought a new house soon after his wife divorced him and took his kids, leaving him a heavy drinker; it was all downhill for him.

Jack bought his only son a brand new BMW. Two weeks later, it was wrapped around a telephone pole, leaving Jack's son brain dead. Jack's remaining days on this earth resembled a zombie effect.

Now, for Paul, it was different. He never touched the money after the bank heist. From time to time, he would look at it with temptation, but he just walked away when he acknowledge the evil it possessed, and from which it had been attained. He still had his wife and healthy kids, and for that, he was grateful. One day, he chiseled a section in the basement concrete. He didn't even open it for one last look. Just laid it in there like a time capsule and entombed it with cement. A couple tears dripped from his cheek and, with his index finger, he made an image of a crucifix in the wet cement.

He walked away, whispering "Thank you, Lord," to himself.

I must ask myself... do I somehow fall under this table?

Good bye,
Paul Swist

CPSIA information can be obtained at www.ICGtesting.com
Printed in the USA
BVOW03s0443031014

369374BV00006B/22/P